Calling To Our Ancestors

酔心

Calling To Our Ancestors

Edited by Sarenth Odinsson

Hubbardston, Massachusetts

Asphodel Press
12 Simond Hill Road
Hubbardston, MA 01452

Calling To Our Ancestors

ISBN 978-1-938197-13-0

Cover art by Shauna Aura Knight

Printed in cooperation with
Lulu Enterprises, Inc.
860 Aviation Parkway, Suite 300
Morrisville, NC 27560

I dedicate this book to my Ancestors, and to the Ancestors of everyone who submitted to this anthology. Whether of blood, marriage, adoption, or spirit, thank you Ancestors for Your many blessings, and hail to You all. May You always be remembered and hailed.

I especially thank my friend, teacher, and Elder Galina Krasskova for inspiring me to put this together.

Contents

Introduction: Blood, Bone, Adoption, and Spirit

This anthology is a collection of writings and works of art made and shared in devotion to our Ancestors. Its purpose is to honor the Ancestors of the Pagan community, and to share our unique perspectives and practices of Ancestor veneration and worship. Each contributor comes from a different place with their Ancestors, and it is my honor to share that with you. This project began at my own Ancestors' request back in November of 2010, and over the following two years has blossomed because of each contributor's unique addition to this anthology. It is my hope that this book enriches your understanding of Ancestor veneration and worship within Paganism, and inspires those who have not engaged in it yet to reach out to your Ancestors.

There are many different ways of acknowledging Ancestors. Some strictly approach Ancestors as those who are blood-related, and/or adoptive families, and nothing more. Some extend their Ancestors to include those who brought their faith to them, such as their priest/ess, the founder of their religion, and the like. Others extend their concept of Ancestors to include Gods and spirits who they believe had a hand in their existence or who have become (or always have been) part of their spiritual family.

Some of our religions recognize our Ancestors as having the breath of life given to Them by the Gods; according to the Egyptian, for example, the first humans crafted by the God Khnum were given the breath of life by Heket, but in other stories it is Shu who gives this gift. According to Norse mythology, Ask and Embla were found as driftwood, and given the breath of life from Odin. Prometheus, in some Greek myths, was said to have fashioned humans and Athena bestowed on Them Her breath of life. For the Afro-Caribbeans, Olodumare created humanity's bodies, and Obatalá gave humanity their heads. In most if not all of our creation stories, our Ancestors were created and given life by our Gods. We are all in some way descended from our Gods.

Many of these religions may contradict one another in their practices regarding the Ancestors, such as whether all the ancestors are available, whether there is reincarnation, how that works, etc. Creation stories can differ wildly, including the role of the Gods in our creation, or who gives the Breath of Life, or how humans came to be, or which Gods created us. Some very wise and experienced authors in this may contradict each other in their beliefs, because they come from so many differing world views. The purpose of this book is not to parse which of these is right, or which way of worshiping, venerating, honoring, or even viewing the Ancestors is "right", "correct", or "the best". The purpose of this book is to honor the Ancestors, each shared from the contributor's own works, beliefs and experiences. This book is a celebration of our Ancestors, the traditions in which we know Them, and may venerate, worship, or otherwise honor Them. Rather than state outright that there is a single way to do these things, this book seeks to celebrate Them in the many ways people have shared here.

Our Ancestors are everywhere. They are in Fire, Earth, Air, Water, and Ice. They are in our blood and bone. They are in our families, adopted or not, by choice or by *Wyrd*. Humanity has grown from great, deep roots.

This book does not seek to be the definitive anthology, either of Ancestor work, Ancestor worship, or of how we come to understand Them. It is an offering from each contributor to our Ancestors. It is the presentation of a door to those who have never knocked for their Ancestors, and to those who seek that door again.

SARENTH ODINSSON
MICHIGAN
OCTOBER 26, 2012

Honoring the Ancestors: Samhain and Beyond

Galina Krasskova

Many traditions pay special homage to their ancestors—those who have come before us; those who by their struggles, failures, victories, and joys have contributed to the common threads of being that we all share. Honoring one's lineage is the first and one of the most important steps in developing a strong spiritual foundation. It is a place of beginning. We all have ancestors. We can all tap into that connection.

Ancestors may include those connected to you by blood, but also those who, without a blood relationship, were nevertheless close enough to be kin. These are our teachers, mentors, and friends—our spiritual kin. No one lineage is better than another. Paying homage to one's ancestors is not, in any way, shape or form an excuse for racism; rather, it is a means of honoring the process of one's spiritual journey, and honoring those whose actions and lives helped create and shape our own. It means honoring those who shed blood for us, so that we might remember and also learn to craft lives of honor. It is an acknowledgement that we are all connected through the Holy Powers, through the cycle that Hela governs. We honor the continuity of Divine presence throughout the course of our lives. We honor their strength, courage, wisdom, and struggles even as we seek to learn from them.

In the Northern Tradition, we have several different types of ancestors. The word *Dis* (plural *disir*) refers specifically to the female ancestors of one's line. These ancestors are very important because they are guardians of one's luck and one's wyrd. Luck in particular relies heavily on the female line in passing from one generation to the next. (Sometimes the word *alf* (plural *alfar*) is used for male antecedents, but in contemporary Heathenry this is not all that common as it leads to confusion with the denizens of Alfheim, one of the nine holy worlds. So most of us just refer to them as our "male ancestors" ... unglamorous but effective!) One might also encounter the word "wight", an Anglicized form of the Old Norse *vaet* (plural *vaettir*). This is a rather catch-all term for nature spirits, elementals, and land spirits. Some use it to imply ancestors, but that is not its most common usage. The Northern Tradition is an animistic one and these beings—somewhat analogous to what Shinto would call *kami*—are no less important than one's ancestors. So we honor not just our dead, but the spirits of the places in which we live, of our home, of the land itself as well.

One does not evolve spiritually in a vacuum. The strength of one's spiritual House depends on the integrity of one's lineage. By this, I mean being in right relationship with our ancestors. This is attained by honoring them regularly, rightly, and well. One's ancestors and the *vaettir* of our world can assist us in our journey and in our spiritual Work. We can learn much from them, but only if we empower them to act with us.

A house cannot be built without bricks. Bricks cannot be secured without mortar. Paying homage to one's ancestors and the spirits of the land is the mortar and clay from which those bricks are formed. We begin in the physical because we are physical beings. Our own physicality—the sense of touch, of sight, sound, smell, and hearing—are the primary filters through which we experience our world. The first step in growing strong and whole and healthy in this tradition is honoring those who have struggled to do exactly that before us. This process is helped by the fact that many spirits choose to stay as watchers, guides, and protectors.

There are endless ways of making proper offerings. The first step one should take is the construction of an ancestral altar. This should be a separate altar from anything given to the Gods—a simple shelf will do, dedicated entirely to the ancestors. In my main kindred, we have a communal ancestral altar with offerings from each person. It's quite a gathering of energies, because we all come from different backgrounds: Celtic, English, Swiss, German, Lithuanian, Cherokee, African, Italian, Polish. We honor our spiritual lineage too. This means that in addition to those actually related to us by blood or adoption, we also consciously honor those people who may have had a tremendous influence on us; who were teachers, mentors, and guides. For example, my mother kept a picture of Wilfred Owen on her ancestral altar, because his war poetry helped her through a very traumatic time in her life. In addition to the shared kindred altar, most of us also have our individual ancestor altars.

I'm often asked how one should go about creating an ancestor altar and it's really a very personal thing. Creating an ancestral altar can be as much an exercise in creativity as creating an altar to a God or Goddess. Whatever reminds you of your beloved dead can go on an ancestral altar; if you have small objects belonging to specific ancestors and wish to honor those people, all the better. The important thing is that the ancestral altar serves as a potent reminder that these people are still part of one's family and one can still have an ongoing relationship with them.

The most common items to place on an ancestral altar are pictures of the dead. There is one caveat here. It is appropriate to place pictures of the deceased, even if they died as infants, on one's ancestral altar; however, under no circumstances should the picture of a living person be included. This is considered the equivalent of tempting or thumbing one's nose at Death, neither of which are wise courses of action. Offerings may include food, cigarettes, raw tobacco, cornmeal (more often given to North American *vaettir* than ancestors specifically), glasses of water, glasses of wine or other alcohol, and various symbols of our ancestors from farther back in both our spiritual and physical lineage. Any objects belonging to one's deceased ancestors are completely appropriate as are items from specific areas. For instance, my maternal side is predominantly Swiss and German. I have embroidered cloths from Switzerland as altar cloths, stones from Germany, soil from the little town my maternal ancestors emigrated from, and even a 16th century map of that Swiss canton hanging above my altar

If one believes in reincarnation, one might choose to honor relatives, friends or colleagues from past lives. One student of mine believes he had several strong lifetimes as a Roman soldier and those lifetimes left powerful imprints on his spiritual psyche. To honor those who fought and died with him and who were his ancestors in those lifetimes, he kept little Roman soldier statues on his altar. It's as simple as that, though it's vital to remember that an altar is a living, changing thing and there must ever be a consistent flow of energy. Keep the offerings ongoing and fresh. Do not neglect the altar, be it the ancestral altar or the primary devotional one. The altar is a link between the living and the honored dead. It is a pathway that must be walked regularly. In the *Havamal*, Odin cautions us:

> Hast thou a friend whom thou trustest well,
> from whom thou cravest good?
> Share thy mind with him,
> gifts exchange with him,
> fare to find him oft.
>
> – Poetic Edda, Havamal, stanza 44

As much as this holds true with the living, it holds equally true with the dead.

> I am always surprised when I run into Heathens or Pagans who neglect their ancestors. Our ancestral dead are no less than the lynchpin of our spiritual protection, luck and well-being. They are truly invested in our safety and will gladly defend us, asking only for our love and reciprocal devotion in return. Consistency is the key here; they want to be an active part of our lives. Honor them regularly, not just when you need a favor. They gave us life; we owe them our gratitude and respect. Anything less is just bad manners.
>
> – *Laura Patsouris, ancestor worker*

Much of what I know about the proper protocol for honoring the dead came through Santerian colleagues and friends. While our religions were very different, we always managed to find common ground when it came to ancestral veneration. We often exchanged ideas and altar suggestions. Many of my colleagues would set up what they called a *boveda*. Traditionally nine glasses (nine being the number of Oya, guardian of cemeteries) of fresh water are set out to ward off malignancy. Bubbling water would be seen as an indicator of incoming negative energy. Water is pure and feeds the dead, giving them vitality. One colleague (an Oshun's man) told me that if the water evaporates quickly, it is a sign that they are "drinking" it. Sometimes the water will absorb negative energy. An odd white film at the bottom of the glasses indicates that the dead are working on your behalf. While this is not something that is part of extant Northern Tradition practice (in fact, I believe it evolved out of turn-of-the-century spiritualism), it is very potent and useful. I have in the past incorporated elements of the *boveda* into my own ancestral altar to great effect. The water should be changed as often as needed, but at least once a week; always flush it down the toilet, rinsing the glasses four times before refilling them. Do not use them for anything else. For me, this was a really nice way of communicating with my ancestors. It helped me to get started and from there, my ancestors were able to point me in the right direction for them and my practices evolved accordingly.

Regardless of how one chooses to structure an ancestral altar, the important thing is to have and nurture the ongoing relationship with one's dead. So once the ancestral altar is constructed, do not forget about it. The altar will grow and evolve over time as the devotee becomes more and more interactive with his/her ancestors. It becomes a living thing, a living source of spiritual vitality, strength, and protection.

In addition to making an altar, there are many other ways of honoring one's ancestors. We visit cemeteries (especially on anniversaries of a loved one's death), tell stories of our dead, name children after beloved dead, keep pictures of our loved ones. These are all ways of remembering the dead, of keeping their memories alive, of reminding ourselves that they're still part of our families. This is what ancestral veneration is all about; moving those things into the sphere of conscious action and then fleshing them out makes it all the more powerful a practice.

Since our ancestors and the vaettir are part of our spiritual life, it is appropriate to invite them to partake of the energy and offerings of each ritual. Therefore, offerings and calls may be made during services. In our kindred, this is done right after the ritual space is blessed. In many other Heathen gatherings that I've seen, offerings are poured out after the ritual is concluded. Sometimes they are given before the space is consecrated. Offerings of bread and beer are traditional for both vaettir and ancestors, but I have found that both will make their personal preferences known. Remember always that these are individuals, not abstract concepts.

I suggest that in ritual practice, after the space has been consecrated, pour or place the offering down and make a formal statement inviting the vaettir and ancestors to partake. It is also proper to set aside a portion of one's meals for the vaettir and even to set an empty place at table for the ancestors. Walking through a graveyard and reading the names on the graves is a way of honoring the dead in general. I will honor other people's ancestors if there is no one else to do it. (Sometimes I'll take full ancestral feasts to local cemeteries just to be polite to the local dead.) Cemeteries are sacred places. The gateway into them, much like the torii gate marking the passage into Shinto temples, delineates passage between worlds, passage into sacred territory. Maintaining a devotion to one of the Deities of the Underworld (Hela in the Northern Tradition) may also enhance ones understanding and appreciation of one's ancestors.

One way of making proper offerings that is often neglected is just talking to the *vaettir* and to the dead. It's possible to develop a vital, interactive relationship with them and they themselves will be the best guide in how to do this. However, please remember that the ancestors are not infallible. They are not Gods. Be sure to set appropriate boundaries with them. For this reason, I suggest honoring one's own dead only. I do not suggest working with random wandering dead. This can be dangerous. And for

Gods' sake, avoid ouija boards. They tend to attract the most egregious non-corporeal bottom feeders. Just work with your own dead and allow them to guide you first, foremost, and best.

In the Northern Tradition, the goal of one's life is to die well. This is not the outcome of some morbid fascination with death but rather the acknowledgement not only of the natural, eternal cycle of rebirth but that dying well encompasses every part of one's life and involves living well, living each day in true, serving the Holy Powers, crafting something for the future. This is the primary lesson of Hela, our Goddess of the Dead. We strive not only to better ourselves and to grow closer to the Gods but to strengthen the threads of our communal wyrd, to craft something better for those who will come after us. Working with the ancestors in honesty and integrity of spirit is the first step on that path. It's not just for Samhain or Winternights!

To the Ancestors in the Scrapbook

Ashleen O'Gaea

On the simple grey pages of history,
your pictures are framed in unconscious confidence
that someone will remember your names,
and your faces will shadow in another generation's light.

You are young in your pictures
and earnest: you accepted your duties,
lit your candles.

Dearly departed, you are present in us
in the usual course of Nature:
you begat us, you were our primal seas.
Cryogenitors, you are frozen,
your breath and years caught in single crystals
affixed to this page.

You are still real.
But I have so short a memory of you
that the fraction must comprise the whole.
You are real; you are real among
faeries and gods;
you are the muses and ghosts beyond our pale and ken.
You are the few moments of your life
that someone photographed.

You are in them, truly:
these are the moments that eternally reveal you,
reveal what your lives meant.
Our blood courses on.
Flesh becomes photograph, effect becomes legend,
and you are still real.

I too will be real some day,
on the simple grey pages of history.

Spirits Whisper and People Speak

Lilith ThreeFeathers Lewis

The first thing you need to know, in order to understand my story, is that I was adopted. Of course, the story is more complicated than that – it always is, isn't it? The brother of the attending physician adopted me at my birth.

Imagine you are a child sitting in class listening to other children talk about having their mother's eyes or their father's hair. Imagine looking in the mirror probing your own face, wondering what a biological parent would have looked like, questioning if your biological mother was short or your biological father had big ears.

As a doctor, my uncle had interacted with my biological mother; he saw her through pregnancy and labor. Yet he refused to answer any questions about her. He had her medical history, but he would not open it. While I respected his ability to maintain confidentiality, it was frustrating—like a succulent un-tasted fruit hanging on the tree just out of reach.

Throughout my childhood, my adoptive family claimed to know nothing about my biological family. Still, there were moments when the adults whispered among themselves. I overheard tantalizing phrases and wished that they would just admit to knowing something. I loved my family and could not picture having another family, but there were moments when I hovered on the edge, looking at how they fit together. Even though I belonged with them, there was a mystery. Rather than a longing, I felt a curiosity. What they were like as people? What did I inherit from whom? What were their stories? However, I realized my adoptive family would never be comfortable talking about my birth. More specifically, my uncle would never tell me what he knew. And so, eventually, I stopped asking.

Decades passed. Along the way I grew to accept my gifts and talents, including the intuition and precognition that had confused my parents. Frankly, I gave up ever knowing more about those mysterious ancestors, but I never gave up looking for answers to the big questions: questions about destiny, god and reality. Those questions led me on an amazing journey, studying several indigenous paths.

That spiritual quest eventually led me to be initiated into Regla d'Ocha (commonly called Santeria), where I was trained to use my mediumship skills. My religion honors the dead through ritualized gatherings and through a special altar called a *boveda*. It's a simple altar to connect with your spirit helpers and guides. Ancestors, even adopted ones, can speak through a *boveda* too. I was told a *boveda* would help me, but I didn't expect much to happen. For decades I had practiced shamanism, working closely with Spirit—spirit guides, Great Spirit, powerful animal allies, and the energies of sacred places. What could a simple altar do? Since it was expected of me, however, I viewed it as a duty.

I arranged nine glasses of water on top of a white cloth. Some people use only one glass, while many use seven glasses, but I liked the way nine glasses looked and felt. Dutifully, I completed the ceremony to activate the altar, elevate my spirits, and prayed for them in the recommended ritualized fashion. Afterwards, I used a simple ritual to connect with my spirit helpers. Once a week I would prepare an offering of coffee, rum and a bit of food. Sometimes I gave them leftovers or a bit of my meal, but they really liked bread and butter. I would light the candle and pray for my good, kind and helpful spirits. Many times I would smoke a cigar as I prayed, blowing the smoke over the glasses.

As an adult who had been adopted, I wanted to gain an understanding about where I fit into this spiritual system. I hoped by elevating my spirit helpers that my connection to them would be strengthened. Truthfully, as I said before, I didn't expect much to happen, but I continued reading the prayers.

One day I set out the offerings and lit the candle, but I did not recite the prayers. Instead I talked about wanting to know where I came from, and who my biological people were. I spoke about my difficulty interacting within a religion that honored the ancestors without knowing something of that biological lineage. I wondered if I was talking to long-dead relatives whose names I didn't know. Was I connecting to someone or something? In shamanism I knew when an answer was given, but sitting at the *boveda,* I wasn't sure what I was doing. Was anyone listening? After a few minutes with no awareness of a response, I quietly left the room.

A few days later, my uncle called. It was unusual for him to call unless it was a holiday or birthday. Since many of our relatives were elderly, I answered the phone with some trepidation. Bypassing the usual discussions of health and family, he immediately began speaking. "I want to tell you about your biological mother."

I was stunned speechless. He talked for ten minutes and then hung up. I sat astonished, holding the telephone. After so many years, after all of the useless attempts to get information, finally, I knew something. Slowly I realized I had my answer. The spirits of my *boveda* had responded, and I walked upstairs to thank them.

Ancestor Invocation

Michaela Macha

You have sown so we might reap,
you have fought for our peace.
You invented our culture,
gained our rights so we´d be free.
All the things that we take granted
once were won by sweat and toil.

Forebears, let us honor you
by using well your gifts to us!
Ancestors, let our lives
shine forth your works, and build on them;
respect your ash, but more important,
keep and feed your living flame.

October Song

Patrick Dunn

These sere trees with their
shawls of crows, sketch lines
on the gray mist,
singing, in the rustle
and fall of their leaves,
the old song of year's
end: My teachers, like the stars,
shine behind
the clouds, gone from this
soil to fly. Their death's
no bar to love. To shrink from this denies
our root: We rise,
like a crow,
from the bone
white egg of the dead.

Ancestors and Descendants: Building Connections

Shauna Aura Knight

In the fall of 2010, I planned a public Samhain ritual for the Chicago Pagan community. One of my team members was pushing for more work with the Ancestors, and I was pushing for more work with our personal shadows and wounds. Both kinds of spiritual work fit well with Samhain and the Underworld. But once again I found myself faced with my guilty secret as a Pagan leader—that I really didn't feel any spiritual connection to the Ancestors.

I had first been introduced to the concept of "the Ancestors" at a Reclaiming event in Chicago in 2004. A movement had begun within the Reclaiming tradition to invite the Ancestors and the Descendants as well as any Elements and Deities. At the Chicago Reclaiming Samhain ritual that year, we did a great deal of work with Ancestors of Blood and Spirit. I felt grateful for the inclusion of the idea of Ancestors of Spirit as I didn't really have any Beloved Dead that I felt I needed to work with. Our closing energy-raising chant was a moving, harmonic piece by Tari Follett and River Roberts:

History, Mystery, legacy, destiny,
We are the gifts, and we pass it on.
Blood and spirit, of those gone before.
Blood and spirit, of those yet to come.

Despite a phenomenally experiential ritual and a moving chant, it was all just a psychological concept for me. In subsequent years as I began to lead rituals in the Midwest, I kept the tradition of inviting the Ancestors and the Descendants. I thought that, even if I did not have a strong connection to the Ancestors, others might and it was important to provide an inclusive way for attendees to connect to the ritual.

At the time, I saw the Ancestors as an impersonal, amorphous body of wisdom. Though my connection to them was weak, I was profoundly moved by the

Descendants. Those who come after us, those for whom our actions will shape their future ... this was an extremely visceral piece for me, often bringing that emotional "full" sensation to my chest and tears to my eyes. My emotions were partly triggered because so much of the work I do is around trying to transform and heal this world of ours. When I think of all the extinct species, the ruined lands, the pollution causing cancer in small children, I get angry and I weep. I want to make a better world for those who will come after us, and remembering them at ever ritual helps to re-inspire me for why I do the work of leading rituals, teaching workshops, and trying to facilitate personal spiritual transformation.

But the Ancestors ... still that amorphous blob. As I continued planning our Samhain ritual, I reached a compromise that would allow work with the Beloved Dead for those who needed that, and offering spiritual work for those who don't have any connection to the Ancestors or have any Beloved Dead. This was fairly easily accommodated in the style of ritual we offer through the tool of a dual-voice trance journey, meaning that several voices are speaking at once to offer several different experiences with open language. Participants would decide what called to them.

Samhain Ritual

Down through the roots of the World Tree, we led the group to the Underworld, the realm where they could speak to their Ancestors or face their Shadows. One voice led the trance arc inviting people to speak to their Beloved Dead. "Have you had loved ones and friends, Ancestors of Blood or of Spirit, pass on this year, or in past years? Is there a message you wish to speak to them, or do they have a message for you?"

I led the "Shadows" trance arc. "What has been your harvest in this past year? And what are the things that you have harvested that you do not wish to plant for the coming year? What are the things that it is time to release, to let fall to the earth as compost? Here in the Underworld, what are the shadows that you must face in order to become your best Self? What is an old wound you must release?" Later on in the ritual, people spoke the things that they needed to release into the fire. They laid down their old pains in the cradle of the earth.

"I'm afraid no one will ever see me for who I am."

"I'm afraid I'll be alone forever."

"I left Mom … I was taking care of her, and then I had to go home, and then she died."

Losing My Father

My father passed away in February after that ritual; I had been procrastinating going up to see him. He was young, in his mid 50's, but he'd had several medical complications in past years. Ultimately we never knew what ailment he died from. My dad was a hippie mystic philosopher, interested in ancient archaeology and psychic phenomena. My dad, mom, brother and I used to joke that, despite having died in the ER before being brought back, Dad never did get to have the classic near-death out of body experience with the tunnel of light.

I didn't see my father often. But whenever we got together, we'd end up talking about the mysteries of Atlantis, secret artifacts and technology within the Egyptian, Mayan, and other pyramids, as well as Reiki healing, Jesus as Reiki healer, aliens, Edgar Cayce, and all sorts of other interesting conspiracies. Dad was always seeking and believed there was more going on beneath the surface of accepted science, archaeology, and history.

I stayed in Milwaukee to deal with finances, funerals, and clean out Dad's apartment. Actually, Dad would have loved all the strange electronic phenomena that went on in his apartment in that week; random watch and clock alarms, lights blowing out, and a memory stick that wiped itself while working on his memorial program. I felt him very strongly in the apartment, which did not surprise me at all given his metaphysical leanings. Dad wanted to be cremated, and we even found four Egyptian canopic jars for his ashes. Before that, my family and I had the opportunity to say goodbye to him. Without any of the nasty makeup or the toxic embalming chemicals he didn't want, he looked peaceful, just like he was asleep. I'm glad I had the opportunity to see and cry on his body one last time. I had never seen the bodies of any of my grandparents.

Finding My Ancestors

It was about two weeks later that I was sitting in a workshop at Convocation, an annual conference in Michigan. I was attending author Kenn Day's workshop as he spoke about family and Ancestors. Suddenly I felt just as I had at Dad's memorial service—he was standing behind me, his hand on my shoulder. I felt him there with his Indiana Jones fedora and some kind of leather backpack/satchel; for lack of better words, it looked like traveling shamanic gear.

In that moment I felt that he had my back, that he was this visceral, tangible bridge between me and all of my other Ancestors. I finally understood the Beloved Dead in a way I hadn't before, not in my head, but in my whole body, my spiritual being. I even felt a stronger connection to the Ancestors from thousands of years ago, the megalith builders of the Neolithic, the temple builders and astronomers and sacred geometers, or the Ancestors of more modern inspirations. I recall that when I was young, I cried when I heard that Jim Henson had died. It had never occurred to me that Jim Henson, or anyone not related to me, could be a "valid" ancestor. With my dad as the bridge that door opened, and now I find that I can reach out to those who have inspired me.

I had thought that I would never have any kind of connection to the Ancestor spirits that so many others found central to their spiritual practice. It was one of my shameful spiritual secrets. Connecting to my father in the realm of the Ancestors is almost as easy as breathing is now. I now have a guide and guardian who was always exploring the metaphysical edges of the universe. It's a comfort, in a way, to know that Dad finally has access to the answer to all his unanswered questions and mysteries.

I believe that some have an instinctive connection to their Ancestors ... but for some of us, we require the visceral connection of someone we know and love passing on. Any one of us may find connections to our Ancestors in different ways. Your connections to the Ancestors may be through a role model you never met, through a family member, or a good friend who passed away. Each of us has our own road.

©2012 *Shauna Aura Knight*

Messages From the Ancestors

Sometimes messages from our Ancestors come from whispers in visions. Sometimes they come from reading what our Beloved Dead wrote or talked to us about while living.

One month before my father died, he frantically called friends and family. He'd had an intense spiritual vision, a mystical communion and rapture with the divine where he spent two days going in and out of a spiritual rapture. When we talked on the phone about this, he had never sounded so happy. He said he'd been crying at the intensity of love, the feeling of being connected to all that is.

I don't believe in accidents. I fully believe this was the divine's way of spiritually preparing Dad for his passing, and I truly believe he was in a state of what I can only call divine grace, a state of spiritual wholeness.

Cleaning his apartment, I came across many of my father's writings. I never knew until I read through all those painful notes that my father had been trying to achieve that kind of mystic communion for years, and he'd felt like a failure for not being able to "get there". He had been waiting for a clear message from God/the Divine/Ascended Masters to tell him what his path was, or when he was "ready". In the years before his ecstatic experience, Dad felt alone, isolated, depressed, and unworthy. It's wrenching to know that he finally achieved the state of divine communion he'd been trying to get to for decades, only to die weeks later.

Having read his writings, and connecting to him as an Ancestor and guide, I feel that there is a message that my father wanted to bring to the world that he was not able to be the vessel for while living. It is that we each need to do our part to heal our world ... to live our dream, and to live it now. My dad let finances, depression, and fear that he wasn't pure enough hold him back. He felt trapped by his job and by money; he gave so much to financially help out our family, even though he wanted to be free of his job so that he could be a healer and spiritual teacher. Ultimately, my father probably died from the complications of job stress. That stress and hurt was on every page he wrote, reminding me that we each have only so much time to reach for our dreams.

Dad felt that our world is on the brink of disaster—as he put it, on the edge of the same cataclysm that destroyed Atlantis. We have technology and greed without spiritual evolution and compassion. He wanted to see people in a place of spiritual harmony and environmental sustainability, divesting ourselves of the weapons that could destroy us.

If I could pass along one message from my father and Ancestors, it is, "Don't wait." We each have a dream inside of us, and we shouldn't wait until conditions are perfect. Joseph Campbell often said, "Follow your bliss." My dad waited for "enough" money, "enough" time.

I hope that my father's passing will inspire you. Perhaps you will be inspired connect with your living loved ones. Perhaps, like me, you will find a way to connect to your Ancestors, finding that visceral relationship if you don't already have it.

And perhaps you will decide that you cannot wait—not another moment—to reach for your dreams, to create a better world for all our descendants.

Don't wait.

Invocation to the Ancestors

Sarenth Odinsson

Blood and bone
Health and life
Pleasure and power
Pain and strife

Skin and flesh
Hair and head
Strength and knowledge
Struggle and dread

Sperm and egg
Vigor and need
Honor and ardor
Conceit and greed

Breath and spirit
Soul and mind
Wisdom and truth
Betrayal and bind

The good and ill
You gave to me
The soul and flesh
In sanctity

Your names and titles
I remember
Your souls and legends
Live on forever

Honor Through Absence

Wintersong Tashlin

I don't have any ancestors.

That sentence is difficult to write, and I know the very idea is anathema to many people's beliefs and practices. Yet it is the truth. And a hard truth it is, particularly for a spirit worker and a shaman who works with the honored Dead.

It goes without saying that I have parents, and grandparents, and so on. So the question arises of how can I not have ancestors? To answer that question, I have to tell you a bit about who I am, and more importantly, where I come from.

I was raised in the Jewish religious and spiritual tradition. Even today, my Semitic heritage is obvious to anyone who knows what to look for. There is a saying about Judaism, one that has been used by everyone from learned Rabbis through the ages to oppressors who sought the eradication of the Jewish people to a deity I had the honor (and terror) of discussing the matter with: Judaism is a religion of blood. Blood suffuses Judaic laws and traditions, from their practice of ritual amputation, to dietary restrictions, menstrual taboos, and laws about bloodlines, inheritance, and the very nature of what it is to be a Jew.

Perhaps most of all, shared blood binds the Jewish people into a Tribe, connected through the ages by threads of bloodlines and traditions. Faith, tradition, and race all run together to form a broad concept of what it means to be a Jew. To be born a Jew is to be a Jew for all time, this is a foundational idea in Jewry. The concept is so ingrained, that it is not unusual to encounter people who identify as Jews, yet do not go to worship services, or perhaps even believe in the Judaic concept of the divine.

Where all of this becomes relevant is that I was not called the service of the Hebraic god, I serve and worship other deities. The very center of my life violates the most cherished of Jewish commandments. To give you a sense of how monumental this is: of all 613 sacred laws, the prohibition against worshiping a "false" god is one of a tiny handful of commandments that may not be transgressed, even if doing so would save the life of another human being.

In giving myself and my oath to other deities, I betrayed my blood and my Tribe. I committed the most grievous sin imaginable in the eyes of my People, and in doing so, went into an exile of the spirit and soul, if not the flesh. Though my blood may be Semitic, I am not a Jew. I am a broken link in a chain that goes back centuries beyond memory.

If I had to do it all over, I would make the exact same choice every time. It is possible to have regrets without believing yourself to be in the wrong.

All my Ancestors are of the Tribe. As an exile, I have no claim to them, and will not offer insult in the form of praise or worship, particularly in my Pagan ways. The best devotion I can show them is to leave them alone.

In living my life *as* an exile, a broken link, I honor the beliefs, traditions, and wishes of the bloodlines that came before me. In the end, that is all that I can offer, and all that would be accepted.

Cry to the Ancestors

Sarenth Odinsson

Oh Ancestors, grant me a tongue
That I might speak your words!
Oh Ancestors, grant me hands
That I might build up your foundations!
Oh Ancestors, grant me feet
That I may stand tall in your ways!
Oh Ancestors, grant me eyes
That I may see your path!
Oh Ancestors, grant me words
That I may speak to your children!
Oh Ancestors, grant me a voice
That I may sing your songs!
Oh Ancestors, grant me a blessing
That my soul be ready!
Oh Ancestors, grant me ways
That I might reach you!
Oh Ancestors, grant me your Presence
That I may know you!
Oh Ancestors!
Ancestors!
Ancestors!
Bless this life you have given me!
Bless this time in which I walk!
Bless this form in which I live!
Blessings to you, Ancestors!
Ancestors!
Ancestors!
Ancestors!

The *Sancti* of the Ekklesia Antinoou: Group Ancestors

P. Sufenas Virius Lupus

A common triad found amongst followers and practitioners of modern pagan religions, and polytheists more generally, is that of gods, land spirits, and ancestors; such a triad reflects the general classifications of divine beings which are deserving of cultic attention or honors. While I do not wish to suggest the following definitions are infallible or authoritative, the general distinction between these three categories is that "gods" are powers that are trans-temporal and trans-geographical, and are often concerned with particular activities, associations, or spheres of life; "land spirits" are incorporeal but are connected to definite and limited geographic regions, land forms, land features, or locations; and "ancestors" are individual or collective human dead who are remembered for their contributions to their human descendants, both in specific terms and for particular influences or accomplishments, as well as simply being causes for their descendants' very existence. In some cultures and groups (e.g. pre-modern Ireland), there is a large degree of crossover between these three categories, with some land spirits eventually attaining the status of deities who are honored outside of their original locations, or gods who are also ancestor-figures, and so forth. Some types of divine being (e.g. totem animals) may exist in a somewhat interstitial classification, as they have connections to definite and specific physical beings who are limited in time and space (like land spirits) but they can be accessed more widely and are not completely tied to these physical manifestations (like gods).

A somewhat intermediate form between gods and ancestors, however, is the theological phenomenon most commonly known especially from ancient Greek and Roman cultic practices, namely the various cults of particular heroes. Heroes often have a divine parent (like Achilleus, whose father Peleus was mortal but his mother Thetis was a goddess), but sometimes they are "mere mortals" of impressive accomplishments and renown, or are known for having possessed exemplary virtues. Because many people in the modern world use the term "hero" rather haphazardly, and "hero-worship" that results in idolizing Justin Bieber or Oprah is seen as distasteful, the entire concept of hero cultus in modern polytheistic practices often gets little to no attention. Some even think of hero cultus as in some way impious or hubristic, since it gives the equivalent of divine honors to particular figures who were human (whether literally or only mythically). Hero worship is derided and forbidden, while cultus to ancestors (who are rarely singled out and are instead revered as a rather faceless group) is not only permitted but encouraged, and can even be assumed to be a necessary aspect of polytheistic devotion ... just as it often was in late antique Europe in the domestic setting, alongside the larger public cults to the gods ... and *to heroes*!

While just as many (and likely far more) people alive today may want to be like and live like Justin Bieber or Oprah than there ever were in terms of sheer numbers of people in the ancient world who wanted to be like and live like Achilleus, and while certain other things about modern hero worship and ancient hero cultus may be similar (including pilgrimages, souvenir-collecting, and revering of images), the largest difference between these phenomena is that those who were revered in ancient hero cultus were invariably no longer in animate corporeal form. Granted, some shrines to heroes included their graves, or certain objects associated with them, and thus there was a corporeal element involved. But there were no "living heroes" in most circumstances in the ancient world. Some people may also idolize James Dean, Marilyn Monroe, or Elvis just as much now as they may have when those individuals were alive, but this particular distinction is an important one when considering what the differences are in terms of hero cultus (both ancient and modern devotional forms of it) and popular culture's forms of hero worship.

In many respects, one can understand hero cultus as a particular form of ancestor worship. While some heroes were certainly cited as ancestors to particular family lines in the ancient world, heroes are divine ancestors in a more figurative, spiritual, or "ancestors of heart" sense to many people for a variety of reasons. A warrior might revere Achilleus for his prowess in battle, whereas some people might have honored a hero like Eunostos of Tanagra because he was tied to a particular locality which had its safety entrusted to him. Such honors eventually became a characteristic of localized practices. (In a sense, such local heroes bridge the divide between ancestors and land spirits, particularly when the hero concerned is the founder and subsequent guardian of a city or other political unit.) Doing cultus to a hero can be considered, in essence, choosing a particular hero as one's ancestor, for whatever reason one might do so.

A figure who straddles the categories of both hero and deity is Antinous, the deified lover of the Roman Emperor Hadrian, who lived and died in the early part of the second century C.E.[1] His cultus was active for several centuries in both large and small manners after his death in late October of 130, in Egypt, Greece, Rome, Asia Minor, and other locations in the Roman Empire. He was never totally forgotten (nor even totally without worshippers!) from the fifth century through the twentieth century C.E., but organized devotion to Antinous on a widespread basis and in a specifically spiritual manner has not existed in a definite and discernible form until mid-2002, particularly in the activities of two groups. The Ekklesía Antínoou is one such group, founded in mid-2007 after a schism by several of the original members from the initial devotional group that began in 2002. The Ekklesía Antínoou is a queer, Graeco-Roman-Egyptian syncretist reconstructionist polytheist group dedicated to Antinous and other related divine figures. Among this group of divine figures are many gods (e.g. Hermes, Dionysos, Apollon, Silvanus, Osiris, etc.) and goddesses (e.g. Artemis, Hekate, Isis, etc.), as well as some of the *Divi*—the deified emperors and members of the imperial

---

[1] For more information on Antinous, and his particular cultic manifestations as both hero and god (as well as other theological categories), see P. Sufenas Virius Lupus, *The Syncretisms of Antinous* (Anacortes: The Red Lotus Library, 2010).

families—of the Roman Empire, but also a large group referred to as the *Sancti*, "the Holy Ones."

The idea of the *Sancti* has been a part of modern organized Antinoan devotion since 2002. Though there was precedent in Greek and Roman hero cultus and the imperial cult for such an apotheosis, it was otherwise unheard of for a non-imperial family member to be deified after death simply because of close association with the Emperor. Antinous' deification happened historically for a number of reasons (foremost among them his death by drowning in the Nile, which by Egyptian custom automatically made a person divine), but one of the most important ideas that has flowed from his deification is that it is possible for every human being to become divine after their death, and to become more divine during their life through devotion and concerted spiritual effort. Whether this "becoming divine" is simply as another departed ancestor (which we all do, even as "ancestors of heart" if we do not have physical offspring ourselves), heroization, or deification, remains to be seen for each person. Within the Ekklesía Antínoou, Antinous' life and death are taken as exemplary and reflective of divine potential; thus, Antinous' own realization of that potential is also possible for others, and in our opinion has been achieved by a number of individuals throughout history, both before Antinous' lifetime and after it. Such people are known as *Sancti*.

Unfortunately, this notion within modern Antinoan devotion has been one of the most often misunderstood, mischaracterized, and even rejected of any that has come about in this particular spiritual context. Too many people see the term "*Sanctus/Sancta*," assume that it is the same as the Christian term "Saint" (which, strictly speaking, it is!), and then assume that all which applies to the Christian canonization process and the qualifications for such also applies to the *Sancti*. This is actually quite far from being the case. There is neither assertion nor assumption of complete and utter moral perfection for those who are *Sancti*. There is also no requirement of having confirmed miracles attributed to someone who is a *Sancta/Sanctus*, and there is no accompanying belief that the *Sancti* have any intercessory power or can act as intermediaries between individual devotees and the gods. There is not even an assertion on a theological level about the *Sancti* existing in a particular form of blessed afterlife. None of these things are impossible, certainly (with the exception of total moral perfection!), but none are required by any means to consider someone a *Sanctus/Sancta*, or to have a devotion to them. While many of the figures were certainly polytheistic in their own theological outlook and practices, and many are even known to have been dedicated to Antinous, others are from a variety of religions and historical periods and are recognized because of their influences and positive examples.

Further, many people remain unaware that the terminology of *Sanctus/Sancta* has precedent in late antiquity, and thus usage of it is not an adoption or appropriation based on Christian terminology. The term is even applied to a figure who was very likely an associate of Antinous: Lucius Marius Vitalis, a young scholar attached to Hadrian's court who died in his youth, likely a few years before Antinous' death while Hadrian was in Athens in c. 128. [2] In his funerary epitaph, he is referred to as *SANCTISSIMO*, "most holy," the superlative form of *Sanctus*. For this reason, he is known as the "Prince of the *Sancti*" in the Ekklesía Antínoou, with "Prince" here being understood not as a ruler or a junior monarch, but instead as "first" or "foremost." It has seemed all the more appropriate and important to use the terminology of *Sancta/Sanctus* because of its explicit usage for a departed and beloved figure in the immediate context of the lives of Hadrian and Antinous.

Primarily, the term *Sancti* is used to indicate that the persons so designated are held in high regard "in sainted memory." They are people of great accomplishment and importance, in a variety of ways, who deserve to be remembered for their contributions to our lives, whether in

---

[2]See Royston Lambert, *Beloved and God: The Story of Hadrian and Antinous* (New York: Viking, 1984), p. 102; Richard H. Chowen, "Traveling Companions of Hadrian," *The Classical Journal* 50.3 (December 1954), pp. 122-124 at 124.

an explicitly Antinous-related connection, in our spiritual practices and thoughts, or in our lives as queer people.

There are a variety of categories recognized among the *Sancti,* reflecting particulars about their lives and accomplishments. A number of deified mortals and (historical/non-mythological) heroes from the ancient world are recognized among them, including Alexander the Great and his companion Hephaistion, and the Trophimoi of Herodes Attikos—Polydeukion, Achilles, and Memnon.[3] The Emperor Hadrian and the Empress Sabina, as well as many of their *Divi/Divae* antecedents and successors, are also honored, including the Emperors Trajan and Marcus Aurelius, and Matidia Augusta, the mother of the Empress Sabina, who despite never being an Empress herself was given the title of *Augusta,* and to whom Hadrian was particularly devoted in her life and her death, having given her funeral oration himself. Other people associated with Antinous and Hadrian in their lives are also included, such as the poetess Julia Balbilla who was a close associate of the Empress Sabina, and Germana, the freed slave who was Hadrian's wet-nurse (who outlived him!). People who served Antinous as sacred functionaries in his ancient cultus are also included, like Isidorus Didymus, an Alexandrian priest, and T. Statilius Timocrates Memmianus, an Argive *agonothete* ("sacred games convener"). "Holy Innocents," people who were slain wrongfully for any number of reasons (including homophobic violence), are also regarded as *Sancti,* such as Hypatia of Alexandria, Tyra Hunter, Gwen Araujo, Brandon Teena, Matthew Shepard, Scotty Joe Weaver, David Kato Kisulle, and the recent large number of youthful suicides due to homophobic bullying (including Asher Brown, Tyler Clementi, Brandon Bitner, and the far-too-large number of others over the last year). Others, who were activists of various types, and who "died in the line of duty" in some sense, are also regarded as *Sancti,* including Socrates, Marguerite Porete, Jeanne d'Arc, Padraig Pearse,

---

[3]On these, see Jennifer Tobin, Herodes Attikos and the City of Athens: Patronage and Conflict under the Antonines (Amsterdam: J. C. Gieben, 1997), pp. 99-109.

and Harvey Milk. A large number of people, both ancient and more recent, who have written about Antinous or made dedications to him, are also *Sancti*, including the famous sophist Polemo of Smyrna, L. Caesennius Rufus (founder of Antinous and Diana's temple in Lanuvium), Johann Joachim Winckelmann (the father of art history), Oscar Wilde, Montague Summers, Marguerite Yourcenar, and Allen Ginsberg. Important figures for queer spirituality and queer life and history are also included, among them Sappho of Lesbos, Plato, Rumi, Walt Whitman, Edward Carpenter, George Cecil Ives, Alan Turing, Freddie Mercury, Bayard Rustin, and Harry Hay. This group also includes some straight people who were major advocates of queer rights, like Beatrice Arthur and Elizabeth Taylor. A final category includes those who have been in some sense very influential for their spiritual contributions, but who are not directly connected to Antinous or to queerness in some manner, including Diotima of Mantineia, Meister Eckhart, Simone Weil, and Joseph Campbell. There are well over a hundred *Sancti* who are officially recognized in the Ekklesía Antínoou at present.

Very often, queer people in recent history have been alienated from their families because of their queerness, and since modern queer people (unlike many others in the pre-modern periods) have been able to decide not to get married or have children on a much more frequent basis, it is often difficult to find ways in which to honor or connect with the idea of "ancestors" at all. Many do not feel they can contact their immediate (or more remote) ancestors because of difficult family issues and rejection; likewise, having no offspring oneself, one will likely never be an honored ancestor to anyone in the future after one's death. As a result, the appeal of honoring the ancestors is greatly reduced for many queer people. The Ekklesía Antínoou's *Sancti*, therefore, are a way in which the group itself and its constituent members can have ancestors of their own, chosen for their important, interesting, and exemplary lives. As the largest part of the *Sancti*'s membership is of people who were in some sense queer, the collective is in large part a group of "queer ancestors", in many senses of the term "queer", and can provide a very relevant solace and continuity for queer people specifically because they are such, and have shared in that particular experience with those living today, who are both their social and spiritual descendants.

There are some in the Ekklesía Antínoou who do not regard Antinous as a god, or even as a hero, but they do honor him and are interested in him, for whatever reason. The idea of the *Sancti* as ancestors, and of hero cultus as a form of ancestor worship, can even therefore extend to Antinous himself for those people who do not find his theology as a hero or god appealing or relevant.

Particular members of the group may have a devotion or interest in certain of the *Sancti*, but not others, which is perfectly permissible; further, the *Sancti* as a group can simply be honored and revered without having to be particular about the lives or influences of certain individuals among them. Cultic and oracular activity in terms of both individual and collective honoring of the *Sancti* of the Ekklesía Antínoou have proven to be effective, influential, and powerful forces of which those interested in this aspect of practice can avail themselves.

Ignis Corporis Infirmat; Ignis sed Animae Perstat—"the fire of the body diminishes; but the fire of the soul persists!" This short ritual acclamation is sung in honor of the *Sancti* on a regular basis, and has been since 2004, as part of many other rituals throughout the year in the Ekklesía Antínoou. Though the gods are great in their power beyond time and space, and the land spirits are directly responsible for the physical life and well-being which we have, the ancestors of those who once walked this earth and who left us their examples in their lives and works continue on even though they have ceased in animate incarnate existence. The *Sancti* of the Ekklesía Antínoou, under the guidance of Antinous himself, most certainly persist in their beneficial influences and guiding examples for the group's members in areas of life as diverse as spirituality, artistic and intellectual expression, and even in sexuality. May these fires, the *Sancti* themselves, never be forgotten, and may these fires always be rekindled by us, and thus may they never burn out!

Ancestors' Devotional

Patricia DeSandro

By bones and stones
And blood and soil
The thread of life
Through time does coil.

Ancestors live!
They hold the line.
From life to death
The thread they wind.

From death to life
They weave for me
Life lessons gain
Eternity.

Wrestling With Iasius: Healing With The Ancestors

Joy Wedmedyk

I have been a Shamanic healer and practitioner for 25 years. The skills I bring to my practice consist of the ability to talk to the Ancestors and discarnate spirits as a Medium, clairvoyant, clairaudient, clairsentient and empath, with the use of divination, and the other connections I have formed with the natural world. As Shamans we develop connections to everything that exits. We believe everything has a spirit. By developing connections to those spirits we can communicate with them and they can help guide us to healing and wholeness for others and for ourselves.

My studies as a Shaman have centered on the teachings of the Indigenous people of the Americas, Cuba and Africa. My healing practice consists of the tools that I have been taught in these various traditions. These include, but are not limited to, communication with Ancestors and Spirits, possession, soul retrieval techniques, and various types of spiritual cleansings. The work that I do as a healer and the tools I use are chosen on a case-by-case basis depending on the needs of my client.

The heart of my practice involves my work with the Ancestors. By Ancestors, I mean the predecessors of everything on the planet. I also mean our own personal Ancestors, our personal family lineage. Just as parents love their children, our Ancestors love us and continue to guide us, even though they have crossed over. Since they once lived, they understand the trials of life and are the most capable of guiding us through our own difficulties. By defining our existence in time, they give us a sense of our place in the world. Our Ancestors are the ones that know our destiny, and want us to have safety, peace and prosperity, not only on the physical plane, but spiritually as well. The Gods' wish is that we are creative on this plane of existence, and it is the Ancestors that give us the drive and desire to do so, and to fully experience life. Through words and language, the Ancestors help us to receive the clarity that is needed that leads to creative action and movement in our lives.

My work involves reading, checking and perceiving the spiritual frame that belongs to the person. The spiritual frame consists of a person's main spirit guide, guardian angel, Ancestors, guides, guardians and protectors, and any other spirits or spiritual forces that have taken an interest in them and work on their behalf.

The health of the Spiritual frame is directly related to the placement and strength of the Ancestors within the frame. Other than our main spirit guide, or guardian angels and protectors, the Ancestors should be the first spirits that are perceived in the frame. They should be in order, and form a trail that moves back through time. The most recently deceased are the most forward in the frame and then the rest line up behind them. The Ancestors should be directly behind a person. There should not be any other spirits as close to a person as their ancestors are. This direct and unhindered closeness of the Ancestors to us is what allows for clear and helpful communication between them and us. They are able to speak to us and guide us without interference from any other outside forces or spirits that may not have our best interests at heart. . All other spirits that are not Ancestors act as support and work with the blessings of and the guidance given by the Ancestors.

The Ancestors should look clear, healthy, and they should be capable of identifying who they are within the frame. It should be easy to see facial features, clothing, gestures, and to hear them speak in clear language. Their demeanor should be one of calmness. Ancestors that are agitated, angry, displaced or noticeably absent in the frame or in need of something from their descendants are not at rest, and signify an area in life and in the Spiritual frame that is out of order and in need of healing.

When I am traveling and teaching, I am fortunate at times to meet other Shamanic practitioners. During one of my travels I met the Lupinsky family, and we had a conversation about our work. The conversation drifted toward the work that they were doing with their son Iasius, who had been diagnosed with Autism. He was also seeing a homeopathic practitioner. He was in school and received services to help him with speech and educational/learning issues. I happened to ask if they had done any work on checking into or with their Ancestors. They said they had not. This was significant to me, because in my practice I have experienced that children with Autism have a displacement in their spiritual frame and a break within their family lineage.

What is an Ancestral break? It is a missing piece in the lineage of the Ancestral chain. When I view this as a Medium, it literally looks like a gap in the trail of the Ancestors as I view them through time, as though a person or group of people are missing in the chain. I have learned that by healing or bringing wholeness there, by organizing the Ancestors into their correct order and reconnecting the chain in a healthy way, one can bring profound healing to people. When the Ancestors are strong and in order, from recent descendants the most forward in the frame, and the rest of the Ancestors moving back through time, it allows clear communication between the Ancestors and us. It also allows the Ancestors to clearly communicate with each other. When they communicate with each other, sharing ideas and advice, they can then agree on the best support and advice that they can give to their descendants. When the chain is disrupted and out of order, Ancestors can speak out of turn, or even all at once, bringing out unresolved issues, demanding attention on small matters, or lose their perspective on what is truly the best for their descendants, bringing confusion to a person's mind and conflict into their lives. These confusing thoughts and conflicts can begin to manifest as disease, mental illness, addictions, obsessive-compulsive behavior, or even as pervasive developmental disorders such as Autism. The healing of the Ancestors and Ancestral breaks is the first step and a foundational piece for allowing healing and wholeness to manifest within a person and in their life.

So it came to pass that Daniel brought Iasius to me and asked me to do whatever I could for his son.

When I first met Iasius, he was a tall and lanky seven year old with a beautiful smile. He exhibited much of the behavior of children diagnosed with Autism. His speech was mostly echolalia, his body was often in motion, and he had difficulty engaging with people. It was difficult for Iasius to focus on conversations or to follow directions without supervision. When Daniel brought him to me, Daniel was leading Iasius by the arm and his arms and legs were pretty much going in all directions as his body was propelled forward.

I created a space where I could get the information I needed to begin to work on Iasius. Creating this space involves reciting a series of prayers to honor and ask for guidance. I pray to God and ask my good, kind and benevolent Ancestors, guides, guardians and protective spirits to be present. Then I ask for help from the spiritual beings that work with me to bring healing and balance. I also honor and acknowledge all the spiritual beings that help and guide me in my work. This can include Ancestors that are shamans, healers and my spirits that work on behalf of myself and work on behalf of others. I also offer prayers for my client in the same manner. The creation of the space opens up communication between myself and my Ancestors and guides. It also opens up the communication that will take place between my Ancestors and guides and the Ancestors and guides of my client. This is the primary way that I receive the information that I need to proceed with any of my sessions.

Usually when I start my work, I use my skills as a Medium to perceive what is going on with my client by first communicating with the Ancestors and spirits of my own spiritual frame. They get the first look at the situation and give me my first impression by showing me pictures and talking to me so I can begin to understand what is happening with the client. I also ask many questions to make sure that I have clarity about where there may be problems, how the problem started, and what I need to do to bring harmony and healing. I set up a divination system that includes stones, bones and found objects. The client chooses from the objects, lays them down, and then I read the patterns that are formed. These patterns help me to receive an impression about the focus of the healing and also where to begin in the session.

Since Iasius was pretty wiggly, I decided to lay the stones and other objects out on the table to see what he would do with them. Daniel had him count, pick out objects and place them in a separate pile. After a few minutes, Iasius got a little bored and took a penny from the pile and started moving it around the room. We kept an eye on him while I looked at the pattern he made. My Ancestors and guides began to speak through this pattern, and guided me to look at his spiritual frame, rather than continue with the divination session, to see what was going on with him and around him. They said that was where to start the session.

My first impression was that there was a vast amount of white space around Iasius, almost like a visual white noise. I had never seen anything quite like that in all my years of practice. Usually I perceive a gray area around a person. The ancestors and other helpful spirits step forward out of that space to communicate with me. At this point I saw only white noise, no Ancestors and no spiritual frame looked to be in place. My ancestors told me that his guardian angel was present although I could not perceive of him.

Immediately following that vision, I felt a powerful spiritual presence come near me. It gave me the sensation that it wanted to communicate by banging its head on the table and repeating, "I am, I am, I am," over and over again. I had the sensation that I wanted to do that myself. When I asked Daniel if that made sense to him, he said that Iasius did that often. He had even tried to get Iasius to respond to "You are who? Iasius?" but the child never could verbalize anything else except to say, "I am."

At the same time that was happening, I saw an unusual type of movement in the white noise of his spiritual frame. There were three black swirling clouds of spirit energy that flew around Iasius' head. They were flying very fast, vary hard and making it impossible to see anything else.

It was time to regroup.

I returned to the prayers. I asked for clarity and peace, protection and knowledge about what I could do for Iasius.

At this point in the session, Daniel took Iasius to get him a cookie.

Because of the chaos present in Iasius' spiritual frame, at this point I could only get information through my own Ancestors as to what was taking place. Through my questions to my Ancestors and spiritual guides, I figured out that Iasius had three spirits that were trying to protect him. By flying around his head in that way they believed that they were accomplishing that task.

I decided that I would do some physical form of cleansing and protection to help him. In this way I could show these Spirits that I wanted to help them protect Iasius, if indeed they were helpful spirits that belonged in Iasius' spiritual frame. If they were not, it would protect Iasius from those very spirit energies.

I started to clean Iasius by blowing cigar smoke on him. This has a two-fold purpose: it allows me to see the spirits more clearly, and it also strengthens the good and helpful Ancestors and spirits in his frame. This makes it easier to communicate with them. Iasius, having shamans for parents, recognized the cigar and immediately started giggling and trying to duck away from the smoke I was blowing at him. This was to my advantage. He thought it was a fun game and was able to sit in one area and play while I continued the session.

I continued the cleansing by spraying rum on Iasius, which works in the same manner as the cigar smoke. It also allows me to perceive imbalances on or in his body that are from spiritual causes. His giggling went into high gear as soon as he saw the rum bottle. Iasius knew what was coming! Daniel had the task of keeping him in one area so that I could aim better. After much giggling and ducking, and with Daniels help, we got that accomplished. It also gave us some comic relief while we were focusing on so many divergent and challenging issues.

The Ancestors and spirits guided me to mark protective symbols on Iasius' body. The protective symbols allow the client to focus on their own space and ignore the influence of the spirits that are around them. I do this with a white chalk that is made from powdered eggshells called *efun* or *cascarilla*. Spirits tend to be hot, and *efun* can cool down the effects of too much contact from the spirits. When spirit contact goes on for long periods of time, this spiritual heat interferes with the well-being of a person. It appeared to me that the three swirling spirits had been around Iasius for quite a while. I needed to cool the energy to get a clearer idea of what they were and how to proceed in the session.

Iasius was pretty ticklish. We had to do some maneuvering to be able to draw on him. Eventually he settled down while I was marking the protective symbols. I gave him the *efun*, and he began to draw on himself, tracing patterns on his skin of the bones in his body.

The intensity in the room dropped off to about half of the level of what it had been. The swirling spiritual beings backed off from Iasius, enough for me to be able to perceive of what they were. Two of them were definitely helpful spirits that were connected to his spiritual frame. One in particular was one of his Ancestors on his mother's side of the family. By settling down these spirits and allowing them to be in their rightful place in the spiritual frame, my Ancestors were able to convey to me what his Ancestor was communicating. This Ancestor stated that he was trying to help Iasius. The second spirit was one of his guides that was also just trying to help the situation. They both told me that they were trying to protect Iasius from the third swirling energy. It was a being that they were fearful of and did not want near him. At this point I was also able to see Iasius' guardian angel and feel the help and protection that were being offered by this Ancestor, his guide and his guardian angel.

This third being was one that I still couldn't clearly identify. It had backed away from Iasius, but was still swirling in his spiritual frame. I also perceived of a feeling of agitation emanating from this spirit. Based on the behavior of this swirling being, I knew that this was where the main healing needed to begin. Since Iasius' spiritual frame was disrupted by the presence of this spirit, I decided to ask my Ancestors and helpful spirits if it belonged with Iasius or if they felt that it should be removed. My Ancestors indicated to me that it was a spirit that was a part of Iasius' spiritual frame, and needed to be helped or healed in some way. This was where an ancestral break had occurred.

I know from experience that Ancestral spirits can at times become detrimental to a person because they are so intent on communicating their intentions. In their persistence, they become desperate and even aggressive toward their own family members. The other ancestors, guides and protectors will want to push the spirit away, or push it back in its proper place within the family chain, causing an ancestral break. The willingness of the swirling being to back away from Iasius supported the conclusion that he belonged there and was a benevolent Ancestor; in my experience, when a benevolent spirit sees that I am able to help, they will try to cooperate as much as possible so that healing and wholeness are attainable for the person that they are trying so desperately to aid.

I would have to come back to that issue because my Ancestors, guides and helpful spirits told me that there were spiritual attachments on Iasius' body that needed to be cleaned off and removed before we could proceed with the healing of the Ancestor, the lineage, and his spiritual frame. They told me to get some mud to clean him. Thank goodness that I was working on someone whose dad was a Shamanic healer, so the idea wasn't so strange. I asked Daniel to go and get some mud from the puddle in the road.

I began praying again. I could tell that this was going to be difficult, and somewhat different than anything I had done before. There was an attachment on Iasius' legs that needed to be removed. I was trying to get a clear visual or message about the nature of the attachment. Instead, I kept seeing images about Iasius' personal spiritual space. He was literally all over the universe, and his sense of self was minimal. Even though this would be expected—because of the disruption in Iasius' spiritual frame which can manifest as a loss of place or belonging in the world—there was more going on. His spiritual bodies were also not well connected. I noticed that his elemental body was very disjointed, and the elements of fire, earth, air and water, were generally not strong or cohesive. These were areas that needed to be strengthened and rebalanced. I sang and prayed for help from the Ancestors, both mine and his, and everything in the universe, including the Universal Mother. I asked all of creation to please help this child who was in so much distress. I asked for specific spiritual forces that knew how to take the attachments away to be present for the healing. These beings can release these spirits, take them away and keep them from returning to the client.

I started to work with the information that the Ancestors and guides gave me about how to proceed with the healing. I was told to start the mud cleansing on his legs. I started at his knees and began to spread the mud down his legs toward his feet. I could sense that something was being moved off his legs. I kept praying for help and guidance, I sang, and I carefully followed the directions I was being given. As I worked on Iasius, he really got into playing with the mud. It was one of his favorite things to play with and it showed. He was being helpful and engaged in the process by spreading mud onto his legs.

I worked down both legs at the same time. As I got near his feet I realized that something was getting ready to be released from Iasius. When I got to the last foot and worked toward the end of his toes with the mud, I felt the spiritual attachment let go. Just as I was about to tell Daniel that it was released, Iasius looked down at his feet and started waving and kept repeating, "Bye-bye, bye-bye Bogo, bye-bye." Iasius had a big smile on his face. He was aware of what had been attached to him, had a name for it, and was happy to have it removed from him. We both broke out it chills. It was definitely an intense moment.

The rest of the information came to me about how to balance his elemental body. As I had done the earth part of the cleansing with the mud, I then cleaned him with fire (a lit candle) and water and air (smoke). During this part of the session, I removed three other spiritual attachments from his body. These were located around his abdomen and his shoulders. I also received information from the Ancestors for Daniel that included prescriptions for spiritual baths and other cleansings for Iasius. They also conveyed messages about how to help Iasius with his socialization and learning issues. These involved messages about how he learned information and about the structures that would help him learn new skills.

The Ancestors showed me that there were still some smaller, unwanted spiritual forces around and attached to Iasius. I was told to wrap Iasius in a white sheet. This is a technique that allows non-helpful spiritual attachments, usually discarnate non-related ancestors, to move off of a person. Non-helpful and discarnate spirits are attracted to the energy field of a person and see it as a light source or as a place to receive energy. The sheet temporarily fools these spirits into moving toward another light source, i.e. a white sheet, instead of staying on the person. It also gives the client an added sense of his or her own space after experiencing so much healing work.

I am sure you can imagine how much fun it was to get Iasius rolled up into a sheet. He giggled and wiggled and generally had a very good time with the whole thing. We managed to wrestle him into the sheet just long enough for me to spray some rum on him. Then he literally jumped out of the sheet. It seemed like he came out from every direction at once. And of course, he popped out with that big smile on his face.

It was time to go back and get the rest of the information on the third swirling spirit that I had seen with Iasius. I prayed again to my Ancestors, and the Ancestors of Iasius' family, for guidance. I asked them to help me perceive the information that was needed to heal this Ancestral break. My vision moved me back through time, and then I saw him. He was an Ancestor from very long ago. I saw him sitting in a cave that was high up in the side of a cliff. He was sitting in front of a fire. I could see the shadow of the fire on the stone wall of the cave. I could also see the stars sparkling in the night sky through the opening of the cave. He was a spiritually strong and powerful man, a very ancient Shaman.

The only connection he had to Iasius was directly to Iasius. There was no lineage between them, no supporting family of ancestors to strengthen the bond between them. This was definitely where the break was in the Ancestral chain. And it was a very multi-generational break. I was grateful to see clearly what I had been looking for.

The connection between Iasius and the Shaman was all-encompassing. The Shaman was spiritually placed right on Iasius. There was no space between them. This ancestor was literally on top of him. The connection was so strong that the Shaman could exert a remarkable influence over this boy's behavior and actions.

I told Daniel that I was going to try to communicate with this Ancestor. When an Ancestor is this close to a living descendant, it is not aware that it is causing harm. My goal was to get this Ancestor to just back up and let Iasius feel and experience his own life. I could tell that this Shaman had an early, more primitive form of language. I prayed to the Ancestors that we would be able to communicate clearly and understand each other.

I asked the Shaman what he wanted and why he was with Iasius. Iasius suddenly sat very stiff and upright and began to answer in another language. He had become a channel for the spirit of the Shaman. Though he was answering in the language of the Shaman, I could hear his answer in English.

The Shaman told me he was training the boy to be a Shaman. I told him the boy was only seven years old and that was too young to be trained. The Shaman told me that he was the right age. (Well yes, in tribal cultures he was the right age!) Unnerving as that was, I kept communicating with him. I reminded the Shaman that he was causing harm to Iasius, and that Iasius was not ready to be trained. I told the Shaman to look at Iasius in this time and place and see if what I was telling him was true. He looked at him hard for a long time. Iasius stopped talking. The Shaman told me that I was right; Iasius was not ready. He stepped back from Iasius and looked at the wall of the cave. He said he would leave Iasius alone until the shadows of the fire on the wall of the cave told him it was time to train the boy.

I thanked him and ended my connection with the Shaman.

I was able, at this point, to see Iasius' Ancestors and his spiritual frame begin to balance, have order, and come into alignment. They were settled, calm, and clear, and I could see the Ancestral chain begin to get stronger and move back through time, toward the ancient Shaman, without disruption.

The last message I received about Iasius was about his point of reference to the world. Sometimes this is referred to as the "assemblage point". This assemblage point is where all the bodies of a person connect together. The bodies of a person consist of their physical, mental, emotional, elemental and spiritual bodies. Usually this point is somewhere near the person, in a person's physical body or within the field of energy that surrounds them. However, in Iasius' case, his assemblage point was fifteen feet away from his body. This was actually an improvement to how I had perceived Iasius earlier because he was no longer all over the universe. The Ancestors reminded me to repeat to Daniel the spiritual baths they had prescribed for Iasius. I was told that these prescriptions would assist in the process of moving his assemblage point closer to his body and to a more personal point of reference. They also recommended another healing session for him at later date.

On behalf of myself, Iasius and Daniel, I thanked all of the good, kind and benevolent Ancestors, guides, guardians, protectors and spirits that helped with the healing. I also did many prayers of gratitude. I stated that I was done for today and closed down the healing circle. And I prayed for the continued healing of Iasius.

Iasius was tired and sleepy, and Daniel took him home. I went to get myself a shot of rum.

The next day, Daniel told me he was the one that had chosen the name "Iasius" for his son because it means "powerful shaman" in Russian. The name was actually a prayer he had made for his son at his birth. This prayer had called the ancient Shaman forward, to the foreground of Iasius' spiritual frame, to bless, protect and influence Iasius' life. In the future, when the time is right, and the shadows of the fire on the wall of the cave tell the Shaman it is so, he will be fully able to help Iasius. But it was not yet time.

A week later, I called Daniel and asked him about Iasius. He told me that Iasius was looking at objects, pointing at them, and naming them without any outside prompting. These skills were new since the healing session. Within two months Iasius went back to school, and after two weeks the Lupinskys were called in for a meeting about Iasius' progress. Since the end of the previous school year, he had shown much improvement. Iasius could now attend to his environment 75% of the time. He was talking more and had new reading skills. He could follow verbal directions and complete tasks on his own. He could listen to a story and circle the right answer to questions about the story. He could engage in play with other students. His teachers felt that he had made much progress in a short amount of time.

I am very grateful to the Ancestors for all their help and guidance during the healing session. Through their kindness and wisdom, and because they love and care about Iasius, they helped me to be able to give Iasius his sense of place in the world, protect him, and bring him spiritual balance. In this one session, we were able to move him toward healing, integrate him and his spiritual frame, strengthen his Ancestral chain and give steady support to Iasius on his journey in this life.

I am very grateful to have been a part of Iasius' life and a step along his path of integration and healing in this world. It is important to remember how much of our problems are Ancestor related and how much the Ancestors can help us with all the healing that we need to do. I offer honor and praise, love and prayers to the Ancestors who have always helped me in my life and in my healing work. May they always bless, protect, support and guide us in our lives. May they always be strong. And may we always be blessed by their loving guidance.

Calling Of The Ancestors

Patricia DeSandro

Into the mist I call to you!
By light of fire I sing your name!
The blood within like river, flows
Through rock and wood and wind and rain!
Still through the dark we reach for you!
The blood, it speaks to ancient ear.
Heed, Ancestors! Hear our plea!
Our need is strong, come near, come near!

Drum Prayer to the Ancestors

Sarenth Odinsson

You rise in my blood
The pounding drum
Life shares life

You cry in my throat
The wordless song
Voice raising voice

You walk in my feet
The endless trek
Stride matching stride

You grasp in my hands
The ever-present work
Grip linking grip

You echo inside
The shuddering beat
Soul stirs soul

A Practical Guide to the Care and Feeding of the Ancestors

Kenn Day

A daily ritual of honoring and feeding my ancestors:

I kneel quietly before the ancestor altar. The stone effigies of Mom and Dad stand there, with the cedar plank Dad carved a face into, representing all those who came before them. There is a small candle in a glass holder and a pewter bowl that holds the remains of my last offering.

Opening my heart and soul to all those upon whose shoulders I stand, both known and unknown, I reach out and pick up the bell, shaking it gently to make a clear high tone. As I return it to the altar, I begin to recite the names of my ancestors...

Woodford R. Day
Florence Heisman
Thomas Jefferson Day
Ada Whitt
Walter Heisman
Elanore Hazelton . . .
. . . All my grandmothers and grandfathers, I honor you.

I bow deeply to all those named and un-named, touch my forehead to the floor in gratitude. I pour a little whiskey from a flask into the pewter offering bowl on the altar. Sometimes it is water. Sometimes a flower. Whatever seems appropriate.

Now I sit and listen for awhile. I can feel my ancestors here with me, and sometimes they will speak to me. When I feel I have received enough, I bow again and thank them.

I am a professional shaman. Since 1989 I've made my living full time by helping people who come to me to heal the wounds of their souls, bodies and energy. During this time, I have observed many wounds that could not be addressed until the client was willing to look at their ancestors and honor them. The purpose of this short article is to lay out the essentials of what you can do, as a "rugged individualist" of the Post-Tribal era, to connect to the souls of your ancestors, and why this would be a good idea.

Let us take a quick look at the nature of our culture. If someone were to ask you who the most important person in your world is, you would most likely answer that it is yourself. This is the healthy response of any well-adjusted person in our society. We live in a time and place where the individual is supreme. While we may talk about how important it is to be a part of something larger—family, career, spiritual community—we always approach that experience as individuals.

In traditional communities, the individual is just not all that important. Not that each and every person isn't valued and appreciated, but it is because they are a part of that larger body—the Tribe—that they have importance. With this sense of being a small part of something larger comes a profound awareness of how many people stand behind you, in the generations of your ancestors, and how their presence continues to impact you in this moment.

What do we mean by ancestor? In many cultures there are rigid boundaries about who is and is not considered an ancestor. I like to keep it simple. Your ancestors are all those who gave you the gift of life. If they were related to you be blood, and they are no longer alive, then they are an ancestor. This can be problematic for those who are adopted, and certainly the adoptive parents deserve honoring as well, but they are not ancestors in this sense of the word. And they do not belong on your ancestors altar, unless your ancestors invite them and let you know.

Most of us ignore our ancestors at best. At worst, we show them disrespect. When we speak poorly of our parents, when we repeat negative or degrading stories about our grandparents, we stand in judgment of them, which is not appropriate. This cuts off a powerful source of potential support in our lives.

In traditional cultures, it is understood that the ancestors remain with us, in some mysterious fashion, long after their physical death. It is understood that we would not be here without the gift of life that we receive from these ancestors, and so we owe them a tremendous debt that we have no way of repaying. Further, it is understood, that if we just pay some attention to them and stay on their good side, our ancestors are happy to provide us with a flow of blessings, energy and advice from where they sit in the underworld. So why don't we do more to keep this connection open and flowing?

Fortunately there are still ways for us to repair this disconnect and begin to benefit from the blessings they have to offer. Here are some fairly simple and direct steps anyone can take in this direction.

1) Set up an ancestor altar in your living space. This is a small table or other surface area that is separate from any other use. It should be kept clean and receive regular attention. Place something on the altar to represent both mother and father's sides of your family and also something to symbolize those ancestors whose names have been forgotten over time. Add a small bowl or dish to place offerings in and perhaps a candle.

2) Make regular offerings. Regular doesn't have to mean daily, though that is best. Offerings can be anything from water to whiskey, raw meat to flowers, incense to tobacco. The idea is to offer something that you believe your ancestors will appreciate and feel honored by. Obviously, don't offer something that would offend them. The offerings should be placed on the altar and should be removed before they become stale or rotten. When they are removed, the offerings should be disposed of in a respectful manner. If possible, they should be released into a natural source of water, burned in a sacred fire, poured out beneath a mature tree, or at the very least returned to the earth.

3) In addition to offerings, your ancestors appreciate being acknowledged and honored out loud. Spirits in general enjoy being summoned with bells, rattles, drums and such. Calling out the names of those ancestors who are known is always a good move, as is a clear statement of gratitude.

After making offerings, it's often a good idea to spend a little time just opening—being receptive to any messages the ancestors may offer you. A simple means of divination comes in handy in this as well, something that allows you to check out what you are hearing. If you feel that they are trying to tell you something more complex and you are not getting it, a visit to a good seer would be in order.

What can our ancestors do for us? Perhaps the idea of being in the flow of life affirming energy and blessings isn't enough of a reason for you to go to all the trouble of setting up an ancestor altar. Once you have established a good relationship with them, you can ask their help for everything from finding your misplaced cellphone to getting a new job. But this doesn't work so well if you only go to them when you need something.

Consider the natural relationship between generations within a family. The children of the family—barring trauma, distance or other distortions of the natural order—are the treasure of the family. The parents devote most of their resources to supporting, nurturing and providing for them. The grandparents dote on them, as do all the living relatives who have any opportunity to do so. Now, take away the division of death. Look at all those generations of Grandmothers and Grandfathers standing behind the living. These all love and want to add their blessings to the life of the children as well. And to all of those who stand behind you, you are that child. The ancestors who respond to your offerings will treat you in the way ancestors always treat their descendants. They will watch out for you, offering protection, guidance and suggestions where needed.

The feeling of all these ancestors standing behind you and smiling their love forward to you is powerful, supportive and energizing. You no longer have the feeling that you are having to wage life's battles all on your own. You also know that they are looking over your shoulder should you think about doing something dishonorable.

Perhaps most important, no matter who you are, no matter what your history, you would not be alive today if not for your ancestors. It is this gift of life that makes them bigger than us. This is a debt we can never repay. No matter how you choose to honor your ancestors, this is the root of what we are honoring. The real shift is not in trying to change how things are, but in acknowledging how things are.

What you do with this information is up to you. Our culture places little value on how we treat our ancestors. If you choose to "go it alone", you will be in step with most of those around you. If you choose to walk in step with the generations that came before you, your path will be filled with more joy and abundance through this connection.

I wish you all the blessings and joy—all the gifts your ancestors intended for you.

Spirit of Antiquity

Robert David Michael

The Spirit of Antiquity, like strength,
Lives in a thousand things: in the city's form,
Here in a building wearing white formal robes;
Caught in a grid of streets; there in the length
Of runners' strides within a stadiums walls;
Bright in those lecture halls where thinkers teach;
Where houses white with blue trim flank a beach;
There where statues are set in a lofty hall;
Wherever men walk proud, breathe freedom deep;
Whenever actors on some wide stage speak;
Where historians pore, where musicians meet,
When lovely themes lull minds to wake, or sleep;
Where lofty poetry aloud is read,
Where bread and wine are shar'd, or beauty addressed,
Where votive stones are raised to the honor'd dead.

Be With Us

Sarenth Odinsson

Where Death's road has led you on
I cannot follow yet
But know that within my home
A place for you is set

Whether on the altar pure
Or before your waiting seat
Know that your place is honored
In the reverence that we keep

We invite you back with food and prayer
With water and with song
We recognize you are in us
And we shall carry on

So be with us in all our times
In times of lean and plenty
We cannot count the blessings given;
Who could count so many?

Re-Establishing Connection With The Ancestors

Sarenth Odinsson

One of many tragedies of our time is that we have lost many connections to our past. Whether one looks to agriculture, to handicrafts, to the stories from the past, or even to just knowing basic information of our Ancestors, many of us have lost these connections.

Some of these connections we are happy to lose, and others we lose to our detriment. I, for one, am happy that women are not considered second-class citizens, are able to hold a job, vote, and make their own way without a man. I am happy that LBGTQI rights are in the forefront of discussion in America, and our society is, albeit slowly, moving towards adopting them into full protections that any citizen can expect.

However, I have lost many connections with my Ancestors. I am only recently learning how to grow crops with my Dad, I am rediscovering handicrafts for myself, and I know very little of my family outside of the last generation or two. I am missing some very vital ties back to my older Ancestors, from knowing how they were able to provide shelter, to how they grew and raised their food, to my own genealogy.

Why would I consider these vital ties? Providing shelter is a basic survival tactic, one that many of us, myself included, do not know how to employ. Providing shelter also brings together people, whether they are communities or families. One need only mention a "barn raising" and what instantly comes to mind is a community coming together to build together. When I think of agriculture, I remember the stories my parents told me of how they got up every day before the sun and grabbed eggs, milked cows, and sometimes weeded the crops before heading out to school. They did most everything as a group, as a family. In short, my Ancestors were far more collectivist than individualist, and this seeped into everything they did, even after the Industrial Revolution. It is only the recent generations that have really forgotten how to rely on one another, and with the forsaking of these connections, we find ourselves in communities we barely understand, let alone with people in them that we know.

Handicrafts, whether sewing, leatherworking, woodworking, sculpture, etc. often provided ways of telling stories of the Ancestors, whether through stone sculpture telling myths and legends[1], or quilt-making that brings people together to celebrate the lives of AIDS victims[2]. They can be functional, as well as decorative, and losing these crafts has meant many stories are simply not passed on. So many stories are told through the simple building of a thing, such as the Lushootseed people's construction of their homes[3]. Losing these connections has sundered many people from their own creation stories. We can recreate these with our Ancestors, and make new connections to our future generations. We just need to reach out, learn, and do it.

Agriculture and other forms of self-sustaining lifestyles are ways that many Americans have simply never connected to. There was a time when most Americans farmed. There was a time when most of the human population farmed, foraged, or hunted for their sustenance. Cutting ourselves off from food production has put many of us, myself included, in the thrall of whatever is cheapest to buy and/or make for our meals. By reintegrating our Ancestors' ways, perhaps alongside ways that work better with our modern world, such as permaculture[4]and transition towns[5], we can reconnect not just to Them, but to the *landvaettir* as well in a deep way. As much if not more than barn raising and similar practices, the growing and harvesting of food brought communities together. It helped to feed the heart as well as the body and soul.

There are many reasons to despair of this loss of connections to our Ancestors, but so many more to reestablish these connections. In my experience, when you come to understand your Ancestors you can better understand yourself. We are Ancestors-to-be, the iteration of all our families bloodlines. Our Ancestors are part of our makeup, from DNA to soul. In addressing our relationship to the past, and to our Ancestors, we can be better equipped to *not* make their mistakes, and to take strength from and in their strengths. In addressing our Ancestors, we can also better address ourselves. In addressing our Ancestors' wrongs, we can heal old hurts, and teach our children and those who share this world with us better ways of being. By reaching back we can relearn old skills that will help us survive both in our everyday life, and in times of trial. One of the best things, in my view, that results from reintegrating one's Ancestors into their life is all the learning you can do. For the Ancestors, in my experience, it is the relationships they forge anew with you, and the ways of passing Themselves onto the next generation in ways that may have long been denied to Them. Whether you are doing basic genealogy research, or integrating Ancestor worship and veneration into your everyday practice, each reach back brings Them that much closer.

I am not for a moment saying that those who have left from abusive family situations must reestablish those connections in the flesh. I am not even saying that they should do that in the spirit; that decision is between them, their Ancestors, Gods, and other spirits with whom they work. Yet it may be helpful to perform elevations with their Ancestors, helping Them rise out of past pain and anguish. Again, that is a decision up to each person, their Ancestors, Gods, and spirits.

Losing our Ancestors' connection creates a hole in our lives. It is not knowing where we come from. It is not knowing where we've been, or how we came from there to here. It is a vacuum which will fill itself where it can, in a search for identity. Taking nothing away from all humans having the same Ancestor, Mitochondrial Eve[6],our more recent Ancestors, even those from a thousand or better years ago, inform our lives in deeply intimate ways. How has your ancestry shaped your life?

My great-grandfather came to America during World War I when he could hear boat guns off the shore. He could have stayed in the Netherlands, and rather than become a citizen of America he could have stayed a Dutch citizen. I can't begin to think of how very different my life might be if he had not gotten on the *Rijndam* on April 14th, 1916, leaving the only home he knew, and sailed into Ellis Island on May 3rd, 1916. Yet this is only one of thousands of stories that distilled into me.

Each and every one of us is a distillation of these stories, legends, myths, truths. Reconnecting to a story helps to fill a hole in my memory, my understanding of where I come from and what has happened so that I am here. Listening to my Ancestors in meditation and prayer has helped fill others, brought lessons on how to do things, such as making a fire, into my life. The Ancestors can reach out to us, as surely as we can reach to Them. Whether we recognize Them reaching out to us is another story. Some of the many ways Ancestors can reach out to us is by giving us a feeling of Their presence, reaching to us through dreams, working with us in our magic and other spiritual work, helping to effect change in subtler ways (i.e. "coincidence", coming into contact with their graves/things by chance, etc.), a story of Theirs being told, or even inheriting things from Them. Our Ancestors can use each of these ways, and more to grab our attention, give us a clue, communicate with us.

The biggest challenge I faced when I started seeking out my Ancestors was reaching out at all. In most of America, even mentioning you want to speak with your Ancestors will get you odd looks, if not outright anger. In this Protestant-dominated discourse on religion, it is sometimes difficult to talk about religious and/or spiritual experiences, let alone actively seek them. Yet seeking our Ancestors *is such* an experience, even if it is not Earth-shattering. It leads us back, and by following the paths back to Them, we can follow new paths forward. We can invite Them along, or They can come as They will, with us on our journey through life. Simply sitting and meditating, perhaps with a photograph, or looking through old records can be connective. It can be a walk through the forest in contemplation of our Ancestors, it can be building a fire. There are innumerable ways to invite our Ancestors into our lives. We just need to invite Them. Even if we don't recognize all the faces, voices, or figures, They will come, and They will work with us to understand Them.

Sources:

[1] American Indian Sculpture, Carving, and Figurines. Native Languages of the Americas. Last revised 2011, http://www.native-languages.org/help.htm.

[2] The Aids Memorial Quilt. The NAMES Project Foundation. Last revised 2011, http://www.aidsquilt.org/.

[3] "Weaving a Life Together: Body, House, Community, Cosmos'. The Lushootseed Peoples of Puget Sound Country." Thrush, Coll-Peter. University of Washington, University of Libraries. Last revised 2012, http://content.lib.washington.edu/aipnw/thrush.html#weaving.

[4] Permaculture Institute. Last revised 2012, http://www.permaculture.org/nm/index.php/site/index/.

[5] Transition Newtork. TransitionNetwork.org. Last revised 2012, http://www.transitionnetwork.org/.

[6] 'Mitochondrial Eve'. ScienceDaily. Last revised August 17, 2010, http://www.sciencedaily.com/releases/2010/08/100817122405.htm.

Ancestor Worship for the Multi-Ethnic Individual

JoHanna M. White

For many of us in the twenty-first century, our ancestors span continents, races, religions and creeds. I often imagine that if my ancestors from the last 500-600 years were together in a room, fighting would likely break out. There would certainly be many different nations, peoples, and languages represented in that room. The question is how one integrates all these people into a successful ancestor worship practice that does not leave practitioners feeling like they are constantly playing the mediator between different familial energies. This is much more complicated than it sounds. There are many techniques for this practice, and we shall delve into a few of them here. Many of those reading this may have no idea about your family trees or perhaps, like me, you know more than you ever thought possible. If your interest is in understanding who your ancestors were better, I'd suggest elderly relatives, Ancestry.com and any of the many DNA genealogy programs out there today.

In my particular case, my father is a mixed-blood Lakota who was born on the Rosebud Reservation and whose mother was a British war bride from Lancashire. My mother's father is a Spaniard of an aristocratic bloodline and had sugar cane plantations in Hawaii before immigrating to the San Francisco Bay Area. His family tree holds Iberian Cardinals and noblemen. My maternal grandmother's family tree dates back through the Puritans, Quakers and early Scots-Irish Presbyterian colonial immigrants to the royal houses of Scotland, Irish Leinster, Burgundy, Saxony, France, Norway, Denmark and Sweden along with a bunch of assorted knights, ladies, barons, and some assorted indigenous wives (Abenaki, Blackfoot) on the frontier as well. It's as if a thousand years of European political intrigue is active among my ancestors as well as the energetic conflict of the conquerors and Native Americans. The complexity of ancestor worship among people with ancestors from many different cultures is a balancing act of working with spirits and ancestral forces that do not have the same goals or desires for you, their descendant. Within my ancestors I have the conflicts born of mixed Native and European heritage; there are many who also have African, Asian, Polynesian, South Asians and Middle Eastern heritage. This adds even more layers to your ancestor worship practice.

Intrinsic to my own ancestor worship practice is altar building. I have been raised in the San Francisco Bay Area and have been strongly influenced by the Dia de Los Muertos (Days of the Dead) traditions that are active here. My ancestor altars include traditional Dia De Los Muertos Calaveras (skulls) as well as photos of people, reproductions of paintings of famous ancestors, dirt from Scotland, and rocks from various locations. I also include skulls, goddess statues, such as Morrigain for my Irish ancestors, and a doll from the reservation where my father was born. When altar-building for ancestors, think about who would want to be next to whom. Perhaps it would not be wise to put the crest for the O'Shaugnessys (an ancestor of my husband who was transported to Australia in the early 1800s for rebellion against the English Crown) near Aoife MacMurrough and her father, King Diarmat of Leinster, who originally asked the Norman King of England for help against the O'Rourke's and thus caused (in many an Irishman's eyes) the invasion of Ireland, from whom my maternal grandmother was descended. Energetically, wouldn't it be best for those two to be far away from one another? And that is just the drama within the ancestors from a single country! The more cultures and beliefs that you integrate into your practice, the more of this kind of energetic feuding you may see.

Perhaps this is a personally-generated sense of feuding. An internal commitment to peace, social justice and sacredness may be enough to create a new energetic relationship between diverse ancestors who are a part of you. However, this may not work for all of us. Therefore, when designing ancestral altars, dynamics like this come into play. And unlike other practitioners who do ancestor worship or work only around Samhain (Halloween), my ancestor altars are up all year long as I would like the beneficial help of my ancestors at many different times in the wheel of the year. This is part of my personal commitment to work with my ancestors regularly; others must make their own decisions about altar timing, placement and energetic commitment.

Your ancestor altars are *yours* to decide whom to honor. Just because you carry the blood of a certain historical figure in your veins does not mean that you need to honor him or her if you do not wish to work with or get advice from that particular figure. This becomes very apparent to persons of African-American ancestry whose ancestors were raped and exploited by other ancestors. Perhaps such a practitioner would like to find a European ancestor with whom they connect further back than the man that who enslaved their ancestors. As another example, Ireland and Scotland strongly call to their sons and daughters regardless of how the blood of those nations got into our family lines. The love of the land and family that those cultures possessed is obvious in many of us who can trace our lineage back to those countries. Your ancestor worship is part of your practice and while this essay may aid or even assist you, I would encourage you to determine the best course for your ancestor worship practice. However, it is still *your* own practice, and no one else's opinion should influence it.

It is you, after all, that have to engage with these spirits. A golden rule for ancestor worship practices is never doing anything that 1) you do not understand, and 2) you do not feel comfortable with. If you feel negative energy from a particular ancestor, or feel that their influence is causing other ancestors you want to work with to back off, then feel free to not give that ancestor your energy. You are alive, and they are dead; you can only honor so many of your ancestors. I only give energy to those with whom I feel a connection and affinity.

Many cultures have different ancestor-worship traditions and I recommend that you utilize the ones that already exist in your family trees. Chinese ancestors may prefer to be venerated in traditional ways such as with sacrifices of fruit, incense, spirit money or candles.[1] (As I am writing this in mid-August, many Japanese are celebrating the *Bon Festival* where they believe ancestors return to visit the living.[2]) When a practitioner of ancestor worship is trying to integrate ancestors into their ancestor worship practice, it is important to take into consideration how these ancestors would prefer to be interacted with. If your practice is truly going to be a respectful worship of your ancestors, then this must be a primary consideration. The library, elderly relatives and reputable research sites online are all good ways to get more information about ethnically specific practices, festivals and events. I am lucky to live in the Bay Area where many multi-cultural events take place, practitioners in rural or isolated communities may need to work harder to attend events or find information.

People of mixed heritage often feel very conflicted about issues involving cultural appropriation. As a person of mixed Native American and European heritage, I would never profess any kind of great spiritual standing in Lakota (or Abenaki or Blackfoot) traditions. I do not pretend to have great knowledge in Lakota practices, medicine or traditions beyond what I have read while working on a second BA in Native Studies. I know only the small things my father taught me as a girl: prayers before hunting, burning tobacco as an offering, and a belief in animism and spirits. However, in my ancestor worship practice, it is not as important that I have not attended a Sun Dance or traditional sweat as it is that I have an honest desire to pray for and to my Native ancestors.

In honoring your ancestors, it is very important to not act as though we are holy people of our tribal heritage. Cultural appropriation is a delicate subject (even for those of us of mixed race), and like many traditions of Wicca, tribally-specific shamanic practices are an initiatory tradition that is handed down generation to generation. Assigning yourself a "native name" or acting as though you are a traditional indigenous shaman does not validate the positions of indigenous folk. If in fact you do want a relationship with religious elders of your tribal group, pretending to be a holy person of that tribe can permanently bar that door.

As a mixed-race woman living in the urban environment, I try to honor my Native ancestors in the best ways I can. I have done so by supporting efforts to preserve Native sacred spaces near to my home. I have engaged in material support for those protecting Native sacred sites including making sandwiches, writing letters and calling development agencies and government offices. There are many things we can do to help other indigenous folk near to home and throughout the world. In addition, many Native American languages are endangered. Another way that you can honor your Native American ancestors is by learning to speak their language and then teaching it to your children or other family members. No matter where you live in the Americas, if you are a person of Native American heritage no matter how small, if the land of your ancestors calls to you, there are ways that you can protect sacred sites, volunteer in native communities, donate money to native causes, and in other ways honor your ancestors. Tribes are about community, and for those of us whose ancestors left their tribal communities for various reasons, it is important to give back to the communities that are here *now*. In doing this, you are honoring your Native American ancestors in a positive way.

Ancestor Worship means very different things to different people. My altar-building, offerings of items, songs and prayers, and doing work in the community in the name of my ancestors may not be what ancestor worship means to you. To find out what is most effective and comfortable to you, use the resources available through the internet and libraries to discover what others have done in the past and adapt these rituals and actions to meet your needs and desires. Use only those aspects that you feel comfortable with, and discard that which doesn't work for you." In the end, it is only you who can determine what is right and what is wrong and what meets your needs. I hope that this has informed your practice and given you something to think about and ways to integrate a more diverse heritage into your practice. Family trees are exceptionally complicated things, and certainly, I have only touched on a few of the issues that may be apparent in the families of practitioners reading this. There are many great books out there on culturally-specific ancestor worship practices, get out there and read them! The more knowledge you attain, the more you can integrate it into a full and beneficent ancestor worship practice.

Sources:

[1] Bary, Wm. Theodore de, with Wing-tsit Chan and Burton Watson. (1960). *Sources of Chinese Tradition*. Columbia University Press.

[2] Shuji, Takashina. (2010). *The Bon Festival and the "Living Dead"*. Last revised August 19th, 2010, http://www.japanechoweb.jp/editors-blog/jewb007.

The Mother Of All Ancestor Questions

Galina Krasskova

(First published on the Pagan Portal of Patheos.com)

There is one question that comes up again and again when I am teaching ancestor work, or counseling those who wish to deepen their relationship with their honored dead. This is not an easy question; in fact, it's actually three questions in one:

A. How do you honor ancestors with whom you had a complicated and not always good relationship in life?
B. What do you do with ancestors whose actions in life (for instance, like being instrumental in genocide) are actions that you completely disavow?
C. Moreover, what do you do when part of your ancestors were the victims of atrocity, and the other part those who perpetrated those self-same atrocities?

Light stuff, right? These questions are so involved and so very complex even to an ancestor worker like myself that I actually called my colleague Laura Patsouris (without a doubt the most gifted ancestor worker I know) for a consult! We hashed out what we would advise in such a situation and that's the advice that I'm going to give here, but in truth there's no easy, pat answer. I don't know what I would do, really, until I were faced with that situation and did the necessary divination (or, if I weren't a diviner sought out someone to do so for me) and prayed to my Gods and Disir (ancestral guardians, powerful female ancestors) for guidance. Still, this might give you a working game plan, should you find yourself in this situation with no one nearby with which to consult.

Question A

This is actually the easiest of the questions to answer. It's really not all that uncommon a thing. It's important to remember that relationships can continue to grow and evolve and even heal after a relative's death. In a situation where the relationship in life was unhealthy or hurtful, you have a couple of options. You can call upon your other ancestors to help you repair the relationship or you can begin a series of elevations to help heal that ancestor. It might take time, but it is possible to work through a great deal of hurt and anger and to turn such a relationship into a strong ancestral bond. There has to be willingness on both sides though. If the living relationship was so abusive and so hurtful that even contemplating an elevation is a horror, then there is no need to do so. You can always appeal to older, stronger ancestors, to your Disir, to the guardians of your ancestral line (we all have dead who take this role) to keep that person away. What you do depends on the nature of the relationship and its history. There's no one answer here.

Question B

There's a big difference between dealing with an ancestor who may have been personally hurtful in life, or who may have been an asshole (we all have those people in our lines somewhere) and dealing with an ancestor who was a sociopath, a war criminal, the willing participant in genocide, someone who committed a massacre, or who might have been a serial killer, etc. etc. What do you do then?

I have to admit, this question really left me at a loss. It's one that I knew I'd have to address sooner or later but I'd been trying to make sure it was "later" rather than now. Still, people are asking and it deserves an answer. What do you do if, for instance, your grandfather was Josef Mengele?

I'll share my colleague's advice first:

> Most people would do exceedingly well to leave a sociopathic ancestor alone, or if that ancestor starts making trouble, appeal to some stronger members of one's ancestral house to keep the deviant one effectively sidelined. I personally would not honor such an ancestor. Now, if you want to be Machiavellian, and you are someone who engages in some rougher forms of magic, you might be of a mindset that this is potentially an ancestor who

> would be willing to do some very dirty things to your enemies for payment. That is a possibility, though I wouldn't suggest it personally.
>
> - Laura Patsouris

I tend to agree with Laura: healing an ancestor and developing a relationship with an ancestor has to be reciprocal. Unless I were pushed to do so by my other ancestors (or the Gods), I very likely would not honor such a person, or attempt to engage with them in any way. Some traditions even have specific rituals to bind such spirits away from one's ancestral house. Moreover, courting such an ancestor in the hopes of having a willing servant is not only dangerous but stupid. It has the potential to lead to one being attacked by that ancestor, and then fed upon and possibly even corrupted by the lich.

If I were pushed to engage for some reason by my other ancestors, I would only do so under their direct supervision and protection. It **is** possible to heal and restore a line, and it's not impossible for such an ancestor to come to a point of wanting to make reparation, but it would take some convincing for me from other reputable members of my line before I'd go there.

> If trusted ancestors give you the push, or your Gods do, I'd listen. The ancestor in question may be trying to clean up the family wyrd and make amends. If so, I believe we should help … if they are willing to work to fix it.
>
> - Laura Patsouris

Question C

This too, sadly, is not so uncommon, especially in the U.S. Some of you may wonder what exactly I mean in the way I phrased this question. Well, perhaps you have a lot of Native American blood, and also the blood of one of the military men who committed their careers to exterminating them. Perhaps you have the blood of Nazi officers and the blood of Jewish victims. Maybe you share Hutu and Tutsi ancestors. Perhaps you have Native American blood from two different tribes: one that fought the European invaders and one that collaborated. Perhaps you have the blood of African slaves and the blood of slave owners…do you see where I'm going with this? Those conflicts don't just miraculously evaporate once everyone directly involved is dead.

You may be called as part of your ancestor work, to engage with both sides of this ancestral equation and it very likely won't be easy.

> Most people who have ancestors from the African Diaspora also carry some European blood, specifically the blood of slave-owners and rapists. I have this in my own family tree. I also have Native American blood and European blood, which carries with it its own history of genocide. How I deal with it is like this: I do not have an issue with the Europeans in my tree who did not commit genocide and who did not buy, own and rape my great-great grandmothers. I do not and will not honor or acknowledge those Spaniards who owned my foremothers. They get nothing from me. I call them out and say: if you ever want me to give you a thing then you know the debt you owe, and the price is working to make things right, work to heal the damage that was done. Some ancestors are unrepentant, and they are too toxic to touch, and you may have to pick a side if there are branches that cannot be reconciled.
>
> – Laura Patsouris

You may find the same dynamic occurring if one of your ancestors was an abused spouse and the other the abuser, or an abused child and the abusive parent. In fact, you may find that in order to begin untangling these threads and bringing some measure of healing to your lines, you may be forced to go back very, very far, to some of your oldest ancestors, and get them involved. It's OK to call upon other ancestors for help with this. They have a vested interest in getting things right. If the oppressor, abuser, attacker sincerely wants to make reparation, you'll have an easier time of it, but note that does not mean "easy".

Beyond that, just understand you're in for some hard work, work that won't go away just because you might decide to refuse to deal with it.

So that is all for now. You've had the opinion of two ancestor workers on these questions. If any ancestor workers reading this have any experiences with these issues or any further suggestions, we'd love to hear them. should anyone have any further questions about aspects of ancestor work, please don't hesitate to contact me.

Thanks to S. for asking this question in the first place, and a huge thank you to Laura Patsouris for engaging in an after-hours consult!

Ritual for Elevating the Troubled Dead

Galina Krasskova

Ancestor elevation is a sacred practice that is done to help the soul of a dead family member who was troubled or angry or depressed in life, perhaps doing harmful things to themselves or others, perhaps never able to live a happy life due to their own inner demons. By doing this, we aid their souls in finding peace. It is an act of mercy, and can also be an act of emotional freedom for the living, especially if their own lives were negatively affected by that individual when they were alive. It is ironically a lot easier to do this work for someone after they are dead. Unlike the act of simply wiping them from one's life, this practice actually helps the problem at its root.

Begin by laying an altar on the floor. This is done in part because the ancestors are our roots, and in part because during the course of this nine day ritual, we will symbolically be raising the altar and thus lifting our ancestor up. Be sure to place this somewhere where it can remain out for nine consecutive days. If you have pets, that's OK. It's not going to harm anything to have them drinking out of offering glasses.

The altar should be white: white cloth, flowers, candles. Culturally for us, this color still speaks of faith, purity, and spiritual cleanliness. In doing an elevation for a particular ancestor, we are engaging in ancestral healing, in cleansing a tiny bit of mess, blockage, pain, strain, hurt from that particular line. White, representing cleanliness to us, is a good color to use for this.

Set up a picture of the dead person you wish to elevate centrally on the altar. (If you don't have a photo, write their name on a piece of white paper in your best handwriting.) It should be noted that an elevation can be done for a beloved ancestor just because you love that ancestor and want the best for him or her. While they are usually done in the case of troubled, aggressive, unhappy, unhealthy ancestors or conditions, they don't *need* to be reserved only for those cases. The only pre-requisite to doing an elevation is that you must already have a primary ancestral altar and an engaged ancestral practice.

Put out flowers. Prepare a candle, a glass of good, clean, fresh water, incense, and whatever other offerings you wish to make.

When you are ready to begin your ritual, set a candle at each of the four corners of the altar and light them, offering a prayer that fire will cleanse and consecrate this space, making it sacred, making it a place where clear communication may occur between you, the ancestors, and the Holy Powers. Call upon any God or Goddess whose help you might wish in this endeavor. Ancestral work is a very personal thing. It not only involves us and our spiritual connections but specific ancestors and *their* spiritual connections. Regardless of the fact that we are Heathen, Norse Pagan, or Northern Tradition, etc. we may find ourselves called to put representations of Deities our ancestors honored on the altar, or to call upon Them. This is not about us. If you have a grandmother who had a close connection to the Virgin Mary, and in the course of an elevation, you get a sense that you should put an image of the Virgin on the altar, I'd suggest doing it because really, who is better positioned to help elevate that grandmother than the God or Goddess to whom she prayed her entire life? Get over yourselves, people.

Sit in front of the altar (on the floor) and call to the ancestor you are elevating. Light incense, then the main ancestral candle. Begin by offering the following two prayers on behalf of this ancestor (these are the ones I commonly use, but feel free to use others if you wish):

First Prayer:
Hail to the Gods and Goddesses.
Your grace illumines all things.
Your gifts shine forth,
Making fruitful nine mighty worlds.
Blessed are those that serve You.
Blessed are those that seek You out.
Holy Powers, Makers of all things,
Bless and protect us in Your mercy.

Lead us along the twisting pathways of our wyrd
And when it is time, guide us safely along the Hel-road.

Second Prayer:
My Lord and My Lady, my Beloved Ones,
May those You call always hear Your voice.
May I always love You beyond trust and mistrust.
May my surrender be complete and voluntary.
Give me this day the grace of Your presence.
When I fail You of Your kindness,
Permit me to make amends.
Use me and teach me according to Your will,
And deliver me from all complacency.[4]

Third Prayer:
Oh clement and merciful Gods,
Magnificent Holy Powers hear my prayer.
I offer these prayers for the soul of __________,
And for all good spirits
Who wish our prayers and recognition.
Please let __________ know that someone here on Midgard
Is stepping forth to speak for him/her.

Merciful Holy Powers,
And all other good spirits and ancestors
Who might intercede for the relief of this soul:
Grant him/her hope.
Grant him/her the awareness
That he/she is illuminated by the Divine Light,
That he/she is younger kin to the Gods,
Beloved of the Holy Powers.
Let her see those tangles in the wyrd,
Those hurts and imperfections
Which keep him/her away
From peaceful tenure in the realms of Hel,
From rebirth, from renewal.

---

[4] This prayer was originally written by Fuensanta Arismendi for the Gods she loved above all others, Loki and Sigyn, but you can readily adapt it to your own devotional connections.

Open his/her heart to understanding,
Grieving, repentance and restoration.
Let him/her understand that by his/her own efforts
He/she can make the time of his/her testing easier.
Wyrd unfolds always, and living or dead
The power to weave it well is in our hands.
May the Holy Powers and other helpful ancestors
Give him/her the strength to persevere in all good resolution,
To meet the tests of his/her wyrd rightly and well.
May these benevolent and loving words
Mitigate and soothe his/her pain.
May they give him/her a demonstration
That someone in Midgard acknowledges, remembers
And takes part in his/her sorrows.
May __________ know that we wish him/her happiness.

At this point, offer the glass of water to your ancestor. Put your ancestor's picture and the glass of water on a book (cover it with a pretty cloth so it's aesthetically pleasing). Remain meditating and praying for as long as you wish.

When you are ready to end the ritual, you may leave the candle to burn for a bit, or blow it out. Thank the elemental power of fire for holding and consecrating the space as you blow out the four corner candles. Thank the Gods and ancestors and then your ritual is over.

Repeat this for nine consecutive nights. Each night, clean, fresh water should be offered and the water and picture lifted by the addition of a new book. After the ninth day, the picture and offering glass of water can be placed on top of the main ancestral altar.

A few caveats: if the candle or the glass breaks, you should do three things:

- Start the entire elevation over.
- Call upon your disir, and other strong and protective ancestors to guide and watch over the ritual.
- Put pieces of camphor in the water. In traditional folk magic, and in spiritualism from which the concept

elevations originally evolved, camphor is protective. It keeps destructive spirits away.

If the altar is very active, change the camphor every day and do not use the candle. Usually your strongest ancestors will come forward to help with the elevations anyway.

I have found that the dead like to be remembered with food, drink, and offerings, but also with music. It would not be inappropriate to offer music during this ritual. At the end of the whole thing, when the elevation is complete, it is always good to make an offering to all your ancestors, and to make an offering to the Gods upon whom you called for help.

You may do elevations for the same ancestor multiple times. It does not hurt. In fact, with particularly damaged or angry ancestors, or tangled *wyrd*, you may have to. It's not a bad gift to give a beloved and healthy ancestor, though.

Adopting Ancestors

Raven Kaldera

As a shaman in the Northern Tradition, I practice in a sect with a heavy emphasis on ancestral work. This tradition even has a minor goddess of genealogy—Hyndla—and right-wing fringe groups who focus on racist and nearly-racist theologies, a twisting of the ancestral focus. While I found many things about my tradition very beautiful—including, even, its climatic legacy of blood and brutality—I was initially quite put off by the ancestral emphasis. Part of this was due to a desire to separate myself from the aforementioned white supremacists, but part was also because I didn't have much of a relationship with my ancestors. When I tried to reach out to them, I didn't get much of a signal ... and this surprised me, because I could connect so much easier with deities, land-wights, spirits of plant and animal and many other noncorporeal entities. It surprised me because I could see and talk to dead people, and laying ghosts was one of my jobs. It surprised me because my patron deity is a Goddess of the Dead—Hela, whose mark I bear on my arm.

Yet, for the longest time, I heard nothing from my ancestors. Eventually Hela revealed to me that a curse lay on several of my family lines, on both sides—and, indeed, that She had brought my parents together for the purpose of breeding those lines. When I asked to know more about it, She sent me to Hyndla, the Goddess of Genealogy ... and the Lady of Bloodwalking. Hyndla taught me how to bloodwalk, and it has been a staple of my shamanic work ever since.

Lessons Learned From Many Trees

Bloodwalking is a type of trance journey, much like pathwalking or "faring forth", but instead of exploring other worlds (or this one), or some other liminal space, bloodwalking journeys down a specific person's genetic family tree. When I do a bloodwalking for someone—which is usually done with a drop of blood in a bowl of consecrated water and a piece of string—I see their genetic ancestors spread out before me like a huge tree full of lights.

Each light is an ancestral soul, and I see them in my head almost like a video clip of them while they lived. Some, full of power, glow brightly. Some are entirely dark, as if the video was turned off—more about those later. Some turn and look at me, see me walking their Tree for their descendant, and perhaps speak or offer aid. These are what we might call the *disir* in the Northern Tradition—ancestors who have taken it upon themselves to watch over their descendants, and have gained power from this dedication. They can be male or female, although I see significantly more female ones, perhaps because guarding the family culture was more of a female job in older times.

I was afraid to bloodwalk myself, so I practiced on my (non-related) family members and my friends at first. I was amazed at the different paths that a dead soul can walk and manifest. I was also amazed at how, for many people, ancestors would volunteer to help by the dozens. It was as if they were waiting for someone to notice them, and ask for their aid.

However, not everyone has ancestral connections of blood that can be depended upon. When I do readings for clients, sometimes I ask about their ancestral connection. For some people, the message is welcoming—"We'd love to help you!" For some, it is indifferent, and for some—as Wintersong Tashlin enumerates in his essay in this book—the ancestors hold up a hand and say, "Don't even ask."

There's also that not everyone who dies is available to call upon as an ancestor. In my experience—not beliefs, but experience in working with the Dead and the Goddess of Death—some people choose to reincarnate, and they just aren't available to talk to as a Dead soul. I know that there are some theologies which postulate that a soul can reincarnate *and* still stick around in some Deathland to be called upon; I am open to the idea that a human soul can have many, many endings, but in my experience, some souls do go wholly back into the material world and they just aren't there any more to be called upon. (And no, I have not experienced that there is a specific time for a soul to be reincarnated. I've seen it happen minutes and centuries after Death.)

In addition, sometimes an individual who was particularly traumatized in life may require a period of time to heal after death, during which they are not available for comment, so to speak. In my tradition, we speak of them "being held in Hela's womb" or "being in Hela's mound"; the image is of them cradled in the dark and being healed. In practical terms—meaning *in temporal human time*—that healing can take days or centuries. My guess, which is only a guess, is that while a traumatizing death can take a while, a traumatizing *life* takes even longer. In the meantime, they are not available to call upon, because they're busy ... and we need to respect that. (Not that the Death Gods will let us do otherwise; They guard the healing Dead with fierce and implacable shielding.) Ancestors who are undergoing deep healing, or who have reincarnated wholly, show up in my bloodwalking as those dark points, as if the TV screen had been turned off, or the line disconnected.

Then, of course, there are the wandering Dead, ghosts who never even made it to the other side because they are still haunting their old home, trying to put the (long-dead) sheep back into the (long-disintegrated) pen. They will stay that way until they run out of life force and can't find anyone or anything else to provide it (like frightened people), or someone with the Gift sends them on. Another guess of mine is that wandering spirits need a very long time of healing, because being a haunt is pretty traumatizing in and of itself. (I've also run into formerly human spirits who had merged with the spirit of a place and become a kind of guardian in the corporeal world, which seemed to effectively detach them from their ancestral tree.)

For some families, the situation is even more complicated and difficult than a single traumatized or missing ancestor. The tragedies of an era can leave their mark on whole generations of a family. I've bloodwalked some clients and seen entire sections of their family tree in shadow, cast into powerlessness by great tribulations such as wars, famine, poverty, or other awful circumstances that left many, many souls too traumatized to do anything but go away to heal. Entire sections of people's family trees can be "shadowed" in this way, and thus useless to call upon. Even if they are not "in the healing mound" or moved on to a corporeal life, they may have little power. If a Dead soul refuses healing, it can sit around wallowing in its trauma for a very long time, and be too weak to help or even care about descendants. I've seen entire generations of a family who were all some combination of weak and missing, and that shadowed generation sometimes made it difficult for the living individual to contact older generations; it was almost as if there was static on the line from that many missing pieces.

Certainly any ancestor who is weak from trauma might be helped by elevation rituals (one of which is provided in this book by Galina Krasskova), which is a lovely way that the living can help the Dead—*any* Dead. Even the most awful Dead can be redeemed with time; a Mongolian spirit-worker once explained to me that the reason her people revere Genghis Khan as a demigod is because hundreds of generations of Mongolians prayed to elevate his soul to its highest self, while keeping his indomitable courage. If it can be done for Genghis Khan, it can be done for your sociopathic grandfather. However, it's a lot of work, and might not get finished before you're an Ancestor yourself—especially if you've got half your family tree to work on.

Visited On The Sons And Daughters

When I finally got the courage to bloodwalk my own lineage, I laid down and cried afterward. Not only were there large swathes of missing ancestors, there was a horrible shadow over the entirety of certain lines on both sides. I would learn, eventually, that this was a blood-curse. It wasn't the worst one I'd ever see, but it was, unfortunately, not something that I could fix. Apparently I had shamanic blood on both sides of my family, and thousands of years ago, it was promised that children who turned up in my lineage with certain Gifts would be turned over to the Gods and spirits to do this job for the community. If they weren't given to the old man or woman in the hut to be trained up, the Gods and spirits who had made the bargain had the right to punish the parents, and any bystanding family members. (I would later learn that this practice is not uncommon among human/spirit relations in many tribal cultures.) Are the spirits lenient once the people have converted to a religion that doesn't believe in this stuff—or thinks it is evil? Do they give the bargain a pass when there is no more old man or woman in the hut, and everyone has forgotten that such bargains were even made? They do not. They smite, and after several generations the smiting has gone on so long. that it has become the equivalent of a blood-curse, weakening whole lines of ancestors and making them powerless. In life, at least in my family, it manifested as insanity and death.

The fact that I have given my life over to the Gods and spirits, sacrificing myself for Their work, released myself and my only child from the effects of the curse. However, it was not enough to save my ancestors. I consulted numerous deities over the matter, and they told me to shut up and be grateful that it wasn't affecting me, or my daughter. My sacrifice had bought her out, and would buy out her descendants ... so long as she (and they) held to the bargain. You can imagine how well her various boyfriends took this news, when she told them what would happen should they have children with the Gifts. To their skepticism, she would say firmly, "I saw what happened to my grandparents! I'm certainly not going through that." So it is: my cursed ancestors don't talk to me, and I have a hard time getting through to what remains of the rest. (My family line seems to have a strong penchant for reincarnation, and also for trauma.)

Blood-curses can happen for many reasons. Sometimes another human being who has been wronged by one's ancestors can call out for vengeance, and be heard. Sometimes a bargain is made with a spirit, and then reneged upon. Some can be alleviated; some can't—at least by the individual in question. For example, I have a strong feeling that it will be someone's job to fix things for my ancestors, but it won't be me. Sometimes that's someone else's work, and you just have to trust and get on with your life. In all honesty, blood-curses are rare; many more people show up to my office thinking that they are cursed than actually are. I see a lot more of them than the average spirit-worker for the same reason that an oncologist sees rare bone cancers: as a bloodwalker, I'm the specialist who can diagnose, and occasionally treat, the sufferers.

Anyway, my ancestors were silent for a long time. Then, out of my ancestry 1300 years gone, an old man showed up. He was the last full-fledged shaman in my lineage, which will tell you just how long this curse had been going on. He's half Saami and half Norse and twice the shaman I'll ever be. My household refers to him as Uncle Noiade—the latter word is the only Saami term for spirit-worker that we know, and "Uncle" is a term of respect, like "honored elder". His altar has a place of its own in my kitchen—he didn't want to be on a general ancestor altar—and is decorated with ornamental reindeer, his spirit herd. So I do have a strong relationship with at least one ancestor, and when I asked him about the bloodline problem, he said, "Don't you have friends? I have friends. I'll bring some over."

Grafting Onto the Tree

I am aware, as I write this, that many practitioners of other traditions feel that no ancestor who isn't your blood ancestor is worth much at all. Some will discourage people from honoring them, and others will speak disparagingly of such practices. This may be because they are coming from a tribal worldview where nearly everyone lived in small genetically similar groups, didn't mix all that often, and didn't necessarily have that many of the issues that I've described in the earlier parts of this article. There is a lot to be learned from those tribal worldviews ... but on the other hand, *we live now*. We live in a world that is very different, in genetic mixing, cosmological mixing, and practices that affect the soul after death. I'm not going to go into all the reasons why—that would be a book in and of itself—but suffice it to say that many, many modern people have ancestral lineages that are nowhere near as cut-and-dried as those of indigenous peoples, just as many of the diseases that plague us are diseases that we have brought into the world, inadvertently or otherwise. We live now, and we have to accept that. We have to learn about the Ancestors and their problems from *many* cosmologies, not just one—if nothing else, because we *have* ancestors from many cosmologies. If your ancestry is cut-and-dried, great. If it's not, adopting ancestors can be a wonderful and effective replacement ... if it's done right.

So how does one adopt ancestors? My first advice is not to go grabbing at famous people that you think will be particularly tough or powerful allies. Just because you think someone's a rock star doesn't mean that they want to call you. Instead, work your way down this list and see where it takes you. Light a candle for them, give them some food and drink that you think they'd like, and see if they respond. I generally try three times and then give up if there's no response.

- *Ancestors of the Heart.* People whom you knew while they were alive, and loved, and know that they cared about you. This could be stepparents, step-grandparents, family friends, your former housekeeper or babysitter, a teacher with whom you bonded. It could mean your deceased ex-lover or dear friend.
- *Ancestors of the Mind.* People who wrote things that inspired you, or helped you through a tough time. Keep a copy of their words on your altar, and tell them how much those words meant to you. These ancestors can also be people who researched important information which helps you in your job today, or were otherwise intellectual pioneers. They can be someone who kept a diary that touched you across time.
- *Ancestors of the Spirit.* People whose magnificent deeds inspired you in some way. Again, if they don't respond, don't feel bad about it—you might not be the sort of person that they hung out with. They might also be gone on to somewhere else for all you know.
- *Ancestors of Lineage.* These are the people who founded, or had a major part in, a spiritual tradition to which you are deeply committed. I've got one of these—yet another old man from Germany who appeared at a pond sacred to my patron Goddess. He was the last keeper of Her shrine at that pond, until he was murdered by Christians

and the shrine was destroyed. Lineage Ancestors can be very attentive, especially if they care deeply about seeing their lineage go on, and you're it.

- *Nonhuman Ancestors.* Some people have spirits directly in their ancestry. It's not very common, but it happens. During bloodwalking, I see nonhuman lines branching off above or below the human tree, at the point where the interference happened. How does this work? It means that someone nonhuman—a deity, a spirit—possessed the body of one of the mating couple that bore you (or, more likely, one of your ancestors), and you can call on that lineage as well. These do count as bloodline ancestors, but unless they are contacting you directly without you initiating it, court them carefully. They can be an amazingly powerful force in your life, but their presence will definitely change it ... and you, as it will bring out those parts of your nature that are similar to them. More specific to adoption, sometimes nonhuman spirits will reach out and form a connection, and you can ask to adopt them as an Ancestor.
- *Ancestors For Whom You Speak.* (See next section).

Sometimes dead people make the first move. The first ancestor that I adopted was sheer accident. Her name was Elizabeth Bellingham, and I was doing a rubbing of her beautiful brass funeral plaque at a museum. I was fourteen years old, and I knew nothing about her except that she lived in the fifteenth century and died a married woman at the age of 24, probably in childbirth. While doing the rubbing, I was surprised to feel her tentative touch, contacting me. We talked, we formed a bit of a relationship, and she dipped in and out of my life. While she wasn't strong, she obviously cared about me; to this day I am not sure why except that we were both lonely at the same moment, on two sides of life and death. We are both clear that she is not related to me in any way by blood. However, I didn't think of her as an ancestor until many years later, as an adult, when I mourned my lack of ancestors who would speak to me and heard her voice: "What about me? Do I count?" I decided on the spot that she did.

You'll notice, as I discuss this, that adopting ancestors is done on a one-by-one basis, and you don't then just call them "the Ancestors" and give them a cookie. You have specific relationships with specific people, and you honor them all separately. That means that this is a lot more work on a regular basis. You can call on them as a group during rituals, but you'd better honor them separately a least once a year, or they'll get restless and disappointed in you. However, it also keeps you "in the work", focusing and paying attention, so in that way it "forces" you to be less lazy about it than you might be tempted to be otherwise.

Speaking for the Dead of My Tribe

Probably the most powerful "grafted" ancestors are affinity ancestors who have chosen you to speak for them. By "affinity ancestors", I mean this: Is there some great struggle in your life about a trait you share with many throughout history? This could be a disability, or a socially unacceptable sexual identity, or some other huge (and permanent) issue that sculpts your life and identity. The point is that this part of your nature is so integral to you that you have much more resonance with the lives of others who struggled with this identity than you have with your blood ancestry. Often, your life is as affected by their struggles and the path they paved for you as the ones who gave you their blood. (Some people with such identities would argue that the gift of life would have been worthless—they would have killed themselves—if not for the work done by these spiritual Ancestors.) If you are very clear that you are a part of this Tribe, who may not be related but who would recognize each other's lives in some deep way, then you have the right to call on that Tribe as Ancestors. However, when you ask this of them, you are also obligated to work for the good of that Tribe, and to help other living members. It is pretty much agreeing to be some sort of activist in exchange for this ancestral power.

One spiritual form of this activism is speaking for the Dead of that Tribe. Speaking for the Dead of one of these tribes is not about putting words into the mouth of famous people. (The famous people wrote their own words, thank you.) It's about speaking for the ones who didn't have a voice, or who were only mentioned in the stories of others. Don't try to decide what they would have said. Just remind other members of your Tribe that they have Ancestors, and to remember and revere them, and be grateful. This is an especially wonderful thing if those spiritual Ancestors were outcast by their families due to their membership in that Tribe, and/or had no children because of it. Their pure joy in being remembered and care about by the people who are their children in experience is beautiful enough to put tears in one's eyes. (This is another reason I disagree with the idea that only Ancestors of the body matter ... it can imply that if you aren't—or weren't—a breeder, if you didn't have living children who grew up to spawn themselves, you were essentially irrelevant to human existence.)

I will say that one doesn't choose to speak for one of these Tribes. They choose you. For example, one Deaf man went to an Ancestor ritual and was contacted by the Deaf dead, and asked to speak for them. A friend of mine is one of the two Speakers for the Transgendered Dead that I know of; she called on them while running from bashers, and they saved her life ... and then said, "You owe us." The power of these Tribes-Without-Blood can be amazingly huge and effective, but you have to work for it. If the thought doesn't fill you with resolution, if it isn't a positive thing, don't call.

Adopting Ancestors is a matter of concentrating on quality and intensity of relationship rather than quantity. I have found not only power but a great deal of spiritual sustenance from my adopted Ancestors—some from the Tribe for whom I speak, some from a handful of beloved Dead with whom I have relationships. It keeps me in touch with the past in a very personal way, and I am grateful for the support of those Souls.

Oh, and if you're reading this after I'm dead? Don't try to add me as an ancestor. According to my Boss, I'm reincarnating whole—meaning there will be nothing left behind to call upon. So don't worry, I'll be back.

Because You Lived: A Song For The Ancestors

Geordie Ingerson

We live because you lived,
Because you wrote, we have your wisdom.
Your blood runs through our veins,
Your brightest flames our inspiration.
We grew because you cared,
Because you dared to swear survival,
We know the road behind,
The threads unwind, the hope we find, because you lived.

We learn because you failed,
Because you fell to fear and rages,
You walked those darkened roads,
The ones who caged, the ones in cages,
And if we find a way
To greater peace, it will be only,
The price you paid for us
That teaches well the lessons learned because you burned.

We live because you strove,
Because you starved to feed your children.
You worked the earth and stone,
The hearth and home, the fields of giving,
You held them to your hearts
And then released them to the future,
They flew from open hands
To do the same, to form this chain, because you loved.

We live because you lived,
Because you wrote, we have your wisdom.
Your blood runs through our veins,
Your brightest flames our inspiration.
We grew because you cared,
Because you dared to swear survival,
We know the road behind,
The threads unwind, the hope we find, because you lived.

The sheet music for this song was created as a choral piece for a Pagan choir. The melody and higher descant were composed by Geordie Ingerson and the bass descant by Peter Ringo. If you want to sing this as a unison song, without parts, the first verse is sung in unison melody; use that part for all other verses.

Add Soprano Harmony
Melody
Sopranos
We learn be-cause you
We learn,
failed, Be-cause you fell
Sop
failed to see it clear, fell be-fore the
to fear and ra - - ges, You walked
Sop
fear, ra - - ges You
those dar - kened roads,
Sop
walked, roads that bled and
The ones who caged, the ones in
Sop
screamed, caged the o-thers' dreams,
ca - - ges, And if we find a
Sop
ca - - ges, And if

way to great - er
Sop
way to o - - pen souls,
peace, it will be on - - -
Sop
peace be - yond the fold, on -
ly The price you paid for
Sop
ly The price you paid for
us That teach - es
Sop
us to see the pain,
well the less - ons
Sop
this change,
learned be-cause you burned.
Sop
learned the har-dest way, you burned.

Add Bass Harmony
Melody
We live because you
Sopranos
We live,
Bass
We live, you
strove, because you starved
Sop
strove to touch the sun, stars that wheel a-
Bass
strove, and starved to
to feed your chil - dren, You worked
Sop
bove, chil - dren, You
Bass
feed your chil - dren. You worked
the earth and stone,
Sop
worked, stone that builds the
Bass
on stone

the hearth and home,
Sop
wall, home that guards them
Bass
and home,
the fields of giv - - - ing, You held
Sop
all, giv - - - ing, You
Bass
fields of giv - ing. You held
them to your hearts, and then re-
Sop
held, hearts as strong as this, re-
Bass
to hearts strong, re - -
leased them to the fu - - ture, They
Sop
lease them with a kiss, fu - ture.
Bass
leased to the fu - - ture, They

Sop
Bass
flew from o - pen hands,
They flew from o - pen hands like sails un -
flew from hands
To do the same, to form this
furled, same tide,
the same
chain, be-cause you loved.
chain us to this world, you loved.
chain you loved.
We live be-cause you
We live,
We live, you

Sop
Bass
lived, Be-cause you wrote
lived like burn-ing stars, wrote your lines in
lived, you wrote
we have your wis - - dom, Your blood
fire, of wis - - dom, Your
down your wis - dom. Your blood,
runs through our veins, Your bright-est
blood, trace the line of life,
our veins, the
flames our in-spir - a - - tion, We
make the spi-ral hold our in-spir - a - - tion,
flame of in - - spi - - ra - tion. We

grew ____ be-cause you cared, ____
Sop
We grew, cared e - nough to
Bass
grew, ____ cared to
____ Be-cause you dared ____ to swear sur-
Sop
give, dared e-nough to live,
Bass
give and dared to sur - -
vi - - val, We know ____ the road be-
Sop
sur - vive the storm, We know the road be-
Bass
vive. ____ We know be - - -
hind, ____ the threads un -
Sop
hind the fall - - en tears,
Bass
hind the

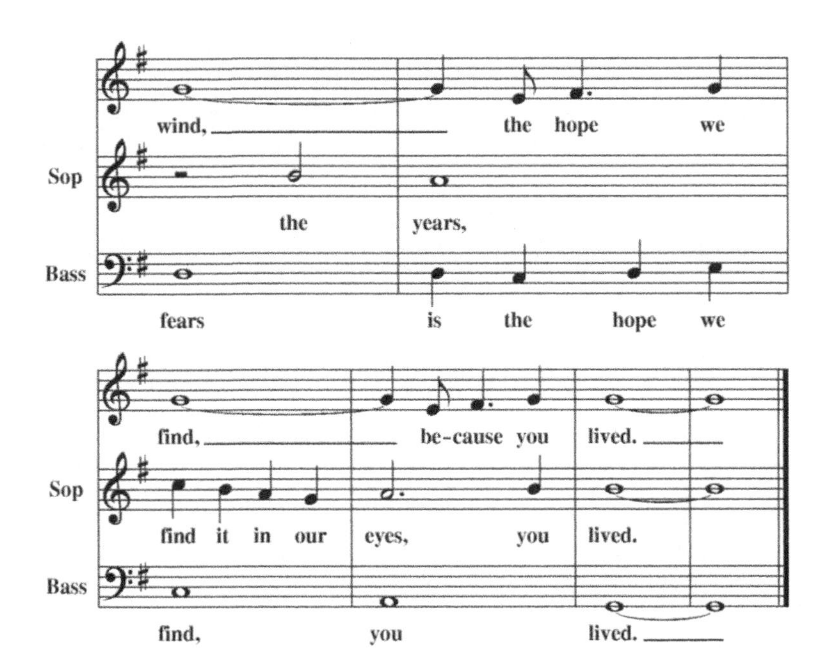
wind, the hope we
Sop
the years,
Bass
fears is the hope we
find, be-cause you lived.
Sop
find it in our eyes, you lived.
Bass
find, you lived.

Call To The Ancestors: A Poem/Song

Sarenth Odinsson

To blood and bone
We sing in stone
In dirt and tree and root
We pray to know
In flame and snow
The breadth of all our birth
We seek your words
In food and mirth
In story and in myth
The ways that you, O Ancestors
Lived in love and frith
We seek you high and low
In Earth and Sky and Life
We seek you in the utter dark
And seek you in the light
We seek you from the Void's old home
From Ice and Flame combined
From the Tree, Breath and Body
Our bloodlines are defined
So come to us, O Sacred Ones
Dance and sing and speak.
So long we've been without your voice,
So long we have been weak,
Come fill us with your blessings,
Come fill us with your songs.
And when we die accept us in
To join the ancient throng!
Welcome me, O Ancestors
Holy Ones New and Old
And through your guidance
Your grace, your gifts
Let the paths of wyrd unfold.

Author Biographies

Ceilidh Chaos has been involved with the Pagan Alliance since 2003 in a variety of different capacities. She is currently President of the Board of Directors as well as Procession Coordinator the day of the event. She is a member of the Renaissance Faire guild the Danse Macabre as well. She lives in Berkeley, with her husband, John, and stepdaughter, Morgan. As a solitary practitioner of faerie, Erisian and animist magick, she considers her work with the Pagan Alliance to be part of her spiritual practice in that she does a service for the larger community of Pagans in this area. She has a BA in Humanities with an emphasis in Art & Education from the now defunct New College of California, as well as two AAs. She is currently working on two degrees at once: a BA from CSU East Bay (Ethnic Studies with an emphasis in Native American Studies) as well as an MA in Instructional Leadership (Education) from Argosy University. Her life goal is to open a Pagan private k-12 school that integrates earth-based spirituality, rigorous academics and sustainability. *www.thepaganalliance.org*

Kenn Day is a working Shaman and a nationally recognized lecturer with over 25 years of practical experience in the healing arts. He maintains an active private practice with his wife at *Body & Soul* in Cincinnati, Ohio and offers a series of shamanic training seminars for those interested in exploring the path of post-tribal Shamanism. He has authored *Dancer of Stones: A Shamanic Road Trip* and is currently working on his second book, *Post-Tribal Shamanism: A New Look at the Old Ways*. For more on Kenn, visit his web site at *www.shamanstouch.com.*

Bona Dea Lyonesse (Patricia DeSandro) is a seer/medium and works within the Wisewoman/Shamanic and Romano-Celtic traditions as an Elder and High Priestess. Also known as the *Stone Seer*, she facilitates healing work for others with her kenning stones.

Bona Dea has been a public speaker, ritual artist and storyteller for more than two decades and has presented

Pagan spirituality in West Virginia, Washington DC area, and many different locations in Michigan and Ohio including University of Toledo and Bowling Green State University. She founded the Circle of the Sacred Grove Temple of the Old Religion in 1999.

She is also a certified hypnotherapist with the International Medical and Dental Hypnotherapy Association and has published articles in *Healthy Living News, Psychic Eye* and *Crow Calls,* and recorded several guided journey/self help CD's. She has also appeared on Buckeye Cable TV and the Sicily Studios podcasts, *On The Edge*. She lives in Erie, Michigan. Visit her site at *mysticbonadea.com.*

Patrick Dunn is an esoteric practitioner living near Chicago. He has published two books on the occult, and one book of poetry. *Postmodern Magic: The Art of Magic in the Information Age* and *Magic Power Language Symbol: A Magician's Exploration of Linguistics* are both available from Llewellyn publications. His book of poetry, *Second Person,* is available through Finishing Line Press.

Geordie Ingerson is a smallholding Vanic Norse Pagan who loves his Gods and the spirits of his land. He is the author of *Ingvi's Blessing: Prayers and Charms for Field and Farm.*

Raven Kaldera is a Northern-Tradition Pagan shaman, herbalist, astrologer, transgendered intersexual activist, homesteader, and founding member of the First Kingdom Church of Asphodel. He is the author of too many books to list here, including the *Northern-Tradition Shamanism* series, *Drawing Down the Spirits* and *Talking to the Spirits* (with Kenaz Filan), *Neolithic Shamanism* (with Galina Krasskova), *Pagan Astrology,* and *Hermaphrodeities: The Transgender Spirituality Workbook*. 'Tis an ill wind that blows no minds.

Shauna Aura Knight is an artist, writer, leader, teacher, event organizer, environmental activist, and ecstatic spiritual seeker, Shauna travels nationally offering intensive education in the transformative arts of ritual, community leadership, and spiritual growth.

She is the author of the ritual facilitation book *Spiritual Scents* and the paranormal romance *Werewolves in the Kitchen*, as well as a columnist on ritual techniques for *Circle Magazine*. Shauna's writing also appears in several anthologies including *Stepping in to Ourselves: An Anthology of Writings on Priestessing* (Goddess Ink), and *Mantle of Stars* (Biblioteca Alexandrina). Her artwork is used for Pagan magazines and book covers, and decorates many Pagan shrines and altars. Artwork is a deep part of her spiritual practice and explores myth, transformation, story, and archetype.

Shauna finds herself on a Grail Quest, seeking the mystical cup that brings transformation and healing to make our world a better place. She is passionate about creating rituals, experiences, spaces, and artwork to awaken mythic imagination and inspire creativity. She is inspired by Joseph Campbell's mythology, Carl Jung's archetypes, psychology, sacred geometry, the design of temples, archaeoastronomy, communication and community building techniques, and shamanic techniques of ecstatic ritual and transformation.

She welcomes questions and conversation about spiritual work, community building, and ritual techniques. *http://shaunaaura.wordpress.com* *shaunaaura@gmail.com*

Galina Krasskova is a Heathen (Norse polytheist) and has been a priest of Odin and Loki since the early nineties. Originally ordained in the Fellowship of Isis in 1995, Ms. Krasskova also attended the New Seminary, the oldest interfaith seminary in the U.S., where she was ordained in 2000. She continues as a guest lecturer and mentor at the New Seminary, and worked there as Dean of Second Year Students for the Academic year of 2011-2012. She is currently the head of House Sankofa, a member of Asatru in Frankfurt (Frankfurt am Main, Germany), the First Kingdom Church of Asphodel (MA), the American Academy of Religion, and the Religious Coalition for Reproductive Choice. Beyond this, she took vows as a Heathen gythia in 1996 and again in 2004.

Ms. Krasskova holds diplomas from The New Seminary (2000), a B.A. in Cultural Studies with a concentration in Religious Studies from Empire State College (2007), and an M.A. in Religious Studies from New York University (2009). She's presented at prestigious academic conferences including those held at Harvard, Santa Barbara University, and Ohio State University. Her Master's thesis, titled "Race, Gender, and the Problem of 'Ergi' in Modern Heathenry" explored concepts of gender roles within contemporary Heathen ritual structure and their impact on contemporary ideological fault lines. She is currently pursuing a PhD in Classics.

The author of numerous books on the Northern Tradition, her *Whisperings of Woden* was the landmark first devotional text to be written in modern Heathenry. Ms. Krasskova currently writes as a columnist for BBI Media's *Witches and Pagans* magazine and co-hosts (with author Laura Patsouris), a bi-monthly radio podcast, Wyrd Ways Radio. While very busy with teaching and school, she does also occasionally lecture around the country on topics of interest to contemporary Heathenry and polytheisms. For more information, please contact her directly at *krasskova@gmail.com.*

Michaela Macha is cofounder of the Asatru Ring Frankfurt & Midgard. She runs the website "Odin's Gift" (*odins-gift.com*) with more than 2,500 Norse poems, songs and mp3s. Her German Heathen album "Skaldenmet" is available at *asatruringfrankfurt.de,* and she's currently working on a Heathen songbook in print.

Robert David Michael (*née* Cerello) was born in Glen Cove, Long Island, New York, and presently divides time between San Diego, CA, USA and Europe. He is an Objectivist philosopher and author. He graduated from Sayville High School, Pomona College, Laverne University's Teacher's program and holds an MA from the University of Virginia and an ESL certificate from S.D.S.U. He has written plays, novels, short stories, songs, screenplays, criticism, non-fiction, verse and poetry for more than forty-five years.

He aspires to be a scientist of the arts and is well-known as a lecturer, actor, singer, author, constitutional theorist, artistic, critic, and teacher.

Sarenth Odinsson, a.k.a. Tim Schneider, is a Northern Tradition shaman, and priest of Odin and Anubis. He has written as well as edited articles for RendingtheVeil.com, an occult ezine, and has been published in *Witches and Pagans* magazine, including the "Spotlight on Pagan Music" series. His passions include writing, reading, drawing, martial arts, theology, religion, spirituality, and sustainable living. Tim holds an associate's degree in Graphic Communication and a Bachelor of Science in Psychology with a minor in Religious Studies from Eastern Michigan University. He can be contacted at *Sarenth@gmail.com,* or through his blog at *Sarenth.wordpress.com.*

Lillith ThreeFeathers works as a medium, shamanic healer, priestess, and writer. Her writings have been published in many magazines and anthologies. Her spiritual and esoteric studies began in childhood. Since then, she has walked both an initiatory path and a shamanic path. After four decades, she continues to be amazed at the miracles that arise from interactions with Divine and Ancient Ones. You can reach Lillith at *lillith3f@gmail.com.*

Joy Wedmedyk (Iyalocha Omi Lasa) has studied Mediumship, Divination, Symbolism, and Shamanism for over thirty-five years. Initiated in Regla de Ocha (Santeria), Native American and African Shamanic traditions, she is an accomplished Medium and Shamanic practitioner and is nationally recognized as a Drum maker, teacher, and Shamanic artist. Her ability to connect to the ancestors opens the way for healing in this world and in the world of the spirits. Joy was a quoted source for *Drawing Down the Spirits* by Kenaz Filan and Raven Kaldera (2009) and a contributing author for *Walking the Path of the Ancient Ways* by Corvis Nocturnum (2012).

Made in the USA
Las Vegas, NV
14 November 2022